Dancing In The Spirit
A Scriptural Study of Liturgical Dance
by

Karen M. Curry

Practical advice and spiritual guidelines for worshippers who are called to the restoration of dance in the Church of the twenty-first Century.

---

authorHOUSE

1663 LIBERTY DRIVE, SUITE 200
BLOOMINGTON, INDIANA 47403
(800) 839-8640
www.authorhouse.com

© 2004 Karen M. Curry
All Rights Reserved.

No part of this book may be reproduced, stored in a retrieval system, or transmitted by any means without the written permission of the author.

First published by AuthorHouse 08/21/04

ISBN: 1-4184-6411-2 (e)
ISBN: 1-4184-2544-3 (sc)

Printed in the United States of America
Bloomington, Indiana

This book is printed on acid-free paper.

All scripture quotations are from the KJV unless otherwise referenced

Table of Contents

I. Preface 1

II. The Tabernacle of David 3

III. Introduction to Liturgical Dance 11

IV. The Call 33

IV. The Temperament 53

VII. The Order 69

VIII. The Priestly Office 99

VI. The Progression 107

Appendix The Tabernacle of Moses 117

Bibliography 119

I. Preface

Just as the look and feel of praise and worship differs from church to church so will dance styles. Therefore, this book is not written as an attempt to standardize the expression of dance in worship. This book is written in an effort to offer practical advice and help to those who wish to start a dance ministry or those who are already a part of a dance ministry and are looking for deeper meaning or for something to confirm their own personal experiences in dance.

You will find answers to questions concerning dance from its scriptural foundations to its appropriateness and mission in churches today. Although there are many styles of dance there is just one Holy Spirit and although we are not able to offer perfected praise in this He will, as in all things, lead us and guide us into God's pleasure. I hope that this book will serve as a tool in that endeavor and will be a blessing to dancers and dance leaders all over the country.

I present to you with humility and with exceeding great joy the things that the Spirit of God has taught me through being in His presence and through serving first as dancer and later a dance leader. I do not profess to know everything about dance as worship but what I do know I gladly share with you! May God richly bless you and your ministry in dance!

II. The Tabernacle of David

*"After this I will return, and will build again the tabernacle of David, which is fallen down; and I will build again the ruins thereof, and I will set it up:
That the residue of men might seek after the Lord..."*
Acts 15:16 & 17

Imagine a rough tent pitched in the wilderness. From the outside, it looks like any other tent; several tall poles support a canvas--perhaps animal skins hanging around the outside. Not a place of elegance--just a rough structure built to house something for a short-term stay. A transitional, mobile, make-do structure.

In contrast, imagine a palatial stone building complete with wooden columns made of Lebanon cedar. Gold furnishings, priests garbed in jeweled robes built with the financial backing of two generations of kings. King Solomon the wealthiest and wisest man who ever lived along with his celebrated father, King David was the financier of this divine estate. So awesome was this structure that after its destruction the old men of Israel wept at the unveiling of its replacement. There was no comparison!

Several temples have been built throughout history in reverence to the God of Israel including; Moses' Tabernacle, David's Tabernacle, Solomon's Temple, Zerubabel's Temple & Herod's Temple. Imagine God, in His divine omniscience, looking back over the annals of time reviewing all of His earthly habitations. The intent is to decide upon a temple to restore for His dwelling.

He considers the temple made by David, the man after God's own heart. David's intent when he pitched the tent was to hold the Ark of the Covenant there for a short time while he prepared to build his God the most palatial temple the world had ever seen. The temple was not completed in his lifetime however; he laid up treasure for his son Solomon to complete it.

God next considers The completed Temple of Solomon. The gold furnishings, the lovely cedar columns... Which would God choose? Again proving that His thoughts are not ours and neither are His ways, God in Amos 9:11 reveals His choice.

> In that day will I raise up the tabernacle of David that is fallen, and close up the breaches thereof; and I will raise up his ruins, and I will build it as in the days of old:
> Amos 9:11

Now what's wrong with God?? We stand scratching our heads considering Him like the parents of a child playing with the box rather than the expensive toy that came in it. Doesn't He realize that tent was only a temporary holding place? The fact is that although the tent was only a tent and a makeshift dwelling, there was something about that tent that God preferred above the wealth, beauty, and awe of the Temple of Solomon.

Structurally, perhaps the greatest difference between the two temples was that Solomon's temple was designed in three compartments much like the tabernacle Moses built in the wilderness of Sinai. The first compartment was the Outer Court, the next the Holy Place and the last the Holy of Holies. The Holy of Holies or the Most Holy Place was separated from the Holy Place with a thick heavy veil. The Ark of the Covenant, which is the earthly symbol of God's Presence, resided behind this veil. Once a year the High Priest was allowed to enter into the Holy of Holies to atone for the sins of the entire nation by sprinkling the blood of a slain lamb on the Mercy Seat. If the High Priest was found guilty of any sin on Yom Kippur, which is the Day of

Atonement in the Jewish culture, he would drop dead in the Holy of Holies. Since no one was allowed to enter behind the veil other than that High Priest a rope was tied around his waist so that he could then be drawn out from behind the veil.

David's temple being a temporary dwelling was not created with the three compartments. David's temple had one compartment—The Holy of Holies. When the people came in to worship, they were ushered directly into the Presence of God. There was no veil. There was nothing separating God from His people. This is key in understanding God's choice. Consider that the expressed purpose God gave for giving Moses the blueprint for the tabernacle was '*that I may dwell among them*'. (Ex 25:8) It was never His desire to be separated from His people. However, it was necessary until sin could be adequately conquered.

Could you imagine having to wait well over 1000 years to be close to the one you love? God had been waiting over a thousand years to destroy that divider between Him and His people. Jesus' sacrifice ended the need for the Most Holy Place to be off limits to every man. In three of the Gospels, the renting of the temple veil is mentioned immediately before or after the Jesus' last breath. His final and ultimate sacrifice enabled God once again to receive worship face to face—as in the Tabernacle of David. How many of us make Him wait longer still for our communion?

Imagine again a rough tent pitched in the wilderness. From the outside, it looks like any other tent; several tall poles supporting a canvas--perhaps animal skins hanging around the outside. Not a place of elegance just a rough structure built to house *God's Presence* for a short-term stay. A transitional, mobile, make-do structure. Now imagine yourself drawing near. Before you enter in there is a noise—a sound. Jubilation, celebration--there's no mistaking it—it is a joyful sound!

Crossing the threshold of the temple you are greeted with resplendent gold, brilliant blue, striking red, bursting amber, and opulent green—rich, luscious fabrics are like confetti in the air, moving in rhythm of the joyous singing and shouts of uplifted voices, instruments and music. Everyone is in one accord waving banners and flags and celebrating. Dancers decked out in majestic materials and hues are leading a procession of people in celebration and jubilation.

As you get closer, you can see that in the midst of the crowd there is a box of pure gold resembling a treasure chest. Atop the box are two kneeling angels with wings outstretched fashioning a seat made of beaten gold. There is a brilliant light in the midst of the angel's wings. Although it should be dark in the tabernacle, it is as bright as day because of the glorious light shining out from the box.

The atmosphere is contagious—you find it drawing you in. The expressions on the faces of the praisers are full of pure joy and abandon. It is almost impossible to just watch. As you surrender to the lure of the praise you are lost in the surroundings. It seems as though hours could pass and the joy and rapture of the atmosphere wouldn't diminish.

But wait! Shhhh the tone is changing. There is a quietening…. a gentle hush over the crowd almost like the lull of waves on the shore. Relaxing, peaceful, serene…. Something deep inside you responds…to a tugging feeling that is not physical. The people around you must be sensing it too. Some begin to kneel, some quietly lift their hands, tears begin to fall like silent liquid, crystal offerings. You notice that some are lying prostrate in total surrender and abandon to—to…. Something—Someone who is worthy… holy. You feel an inexplicable urge to bow.

Dancing In The Spirit

Soft, intermittent unintelligible whispers are heard. Syllables of words that were never before spoken on earth are breathed in muted tones. The peace flows in waves like warm, gentle waves on a secluded seashore. Everyone has forgotten the presence of everyone else except–the holy Presence to which everyone acknowledges in their own personal, intimate way.

Oh, there is nothing like this peace! What fullness! Nothing on earth has ever touched you so deeply before. Like never before you sense that you are connected, indelibly to something greater, you were born for something more. Right now you have found that purpose. —Someone— different. Someone holy is here.

Comfort envelopes you like a warm blanket--comfort for the secret pains that you have never acknowledged at a conscious level. Hurts buried long ago are being uncovered and healed in this Presence. Love that you have always silently, craved fills the holes and voids in your broken heart. You sense words of encouragement, peace, love, and patience whispered but not in your ears. Rather somewhere deep inside you. You, like an unborn babe, can feel His divine heartbeat lulling you into peace and comfort.

Here, lost in His Presence time means nothing. Nothing means anything.... except the passion being birthed inside you. Even as you are afraid to move, afraid to end the experience you unconsciously press your way closer to the glory shining from that mysterious box in the midst of the room, your mind reels *"How can I get closer to this Presence? How can I get closer to Him?"*

One by one the people begin to dissipate. As they leave, another call to praise is sounded in the camp. The shifts change and another group of praisers begins to assemble. A procession of banners and flags arrive. The musicians begin to play and whole progression begins again. As you are ushered back out into the light of day you know that deep within you have been changed—deep within everything is new. Your mind keeps repeating *"When can I come back? Next time I'll get closer. I have to get closer..."*

This, beloved, is worship. That desperate, relentless pursuit that draws you by the delicate strings of your spirit to weekly, daily, hourly press your way closer into that most privileged place. You enter the Holy of Holies thinking *"Maybe He'll show me His face today. Maybe I can touch His heart today."* It leaves your soul hungry no matter how often you consume of Him--you are insatiable. This was the attitude of David, the man after God's own heart. It was the attitude that prompted David to commission singers, dancers, musicians, and other worshippers to worship around the clock in his little makeshift tent.

Without intending to, with only the desire to please the Lover of his Soul, David stumbles upon the prescription for worship that captures the heart of the Almighty. Our nations are ailing with the illnesses of crime, teen pregnancy, drug addiction, hopelessness, and godlessness. We wonder how to make a difference in our communities, how to rebuild our inner cities, how to capture our youth. We wonder how to give hope to crime-ridden communities and how to give life and vitality to our churches. The Holy Spirit is writing today the same prescription today. The call to worship is sounding. The Tabernacle of David is being restored. Can you hear the call? It is resounding in the heart of the worshipers.

The prophet Ezekiel in Chapter 47 tells us about a river of water that flows forth from the Temple of God. The further the river flows from the temple the deeper it gets until the waters are deep enough to swim in. As the river flows everywhere it touches begins to flourish. Ezekiel describes the scene before him as 'a very great many trees' springing forth and the streams and ponds teeming with fish.' This river touches the desert and heals the waters of the sea.

And it shall come to pass, [that] every thing that liveth, which moveth, whithersoever the rivers shall come, shall live: and there shall be a very great multitude of fish, because these waters shall come thither: for they shall be healed; and every thing shall live whither the river cometh.

Eze 47:9

In Revelation 22:1 the Apostle John tell us of a pure river of crystal clear waters of life emanating from the throne of God and from the Lamb. This river nourishes the Tree of Life. For fear that we might in our sinful state reach out and grasp eternal life through the fruit of this tree, our great great grandfather was banished from the garden. (Gen 3:22) In Genesis, the tree is denied us. However, in the Revelation we are reintroduced to the tree again and the river of living water that nourishes it. We are told that the curse is ended and that the tree provides in its fruit and leaves healing for the nations.

Beloved, we are Ezekiel's Temple of God (I Cor 3:16) and John 7:38 tells us that this river of life flows forth from our bellies. That praise, the magnificent, joyful sound is within you. You are the hope, the cure for your house, your neighborhood, your community and for your world.

Together let us endeavor to rebuild the Tabernacle of David. Let our desire be to do this because it is the expressed desire of the Lord. We can pray that we like David; stumble onto the pattern, the panacea, the prescription that will succeed in capturing the heart of God and causing the living waters to flow touching the world with healing life.

III. Introduction to Liturgical Dance

Liturgical dance is the decent and proper expression to God or from God (prophetic dance) through dance using music and choreography that attributes honor and glory to God. It is not enough to be a Christian and dance to any kind of music using any kind of choreography. (In this how would we differ from the world?) This dance, in order to be pure and perfect praise, must from it's origin come forth for the specific purpose of glorifying God. It's main focus is to direct the congregation to God and to encourage them to enter into worship. The focus is not the dancer, not the choreographer, nor the costumer, but God. The preceding will be our working definition of Liturgical Dance.

The Origins of Dance

It is important for liturgical dancers today to have some idea of the history of dance especially so that we can understand that dance is not a 'secular' art form. Dance began in history as a religious expression. It is only natural that sooner or later it return to its origin. As you read this section, please be aware that this is only an introduction to dance history. A separate book entirely would be necessary to do justice to the comprehensive history of the art of dance. Instead I have chosen some major events, dancers and dances that I feel are important to share with you.

History records the first dances as religious rites that were performed in early ancient cultures. In these nomadic tribes, a specific dance accompanied births, deaths, marriages, the marking of manhood and womanhood. Dances were also a preparation for hunting and war and to record history.

Harmony of the body and mind, the Greek ideal, was believed to be promoted through dance. In ancient

Greece (around 500 B.C.) young men and women were taught dance from early ages as a part of their education. Dance was also taught to young soldiers as preparation for battle. Socrates was quoted as saying that the best dancers were also the best soldiers.

During this time, cult worship was very prevalent in the Greek and Roman cultures. One of the other common themes in the worship of these gods was dance--specifically the deities Artemis (Diana), Baal or the Calf God (to whom the Israelites had Aaron erect a statute in Moses' absence), Cybele, the Roman goddess of fertility and Dionysis the lord of wine. The worship of many of these "gods" included human sacrifices, even the sacrifice of infants. The dancing associated with these cultic gods was wild and reveling and many times included orgies and other sexual perversion.

The great Roman orator Cicero once said:

> "No man who is sober dances, unless he is out of his mind either alone or in any decent society, for dancing is the companion of wanton conviviality, dissoluteness, and luxury."

It was this type of thought in the Roman culture that kept dance specifically associated with the foreign gods who had been adopted from the Greek culture. The Romans did see the benefit in the Greek war dance called the pyrrhic that was used to train young soldiers for battle. They adopted the pyrrhic as well as Greek dances for crop planting and funerals.

In the early Middle Ages as people traveled to sell wares or to visit a fair, dances were held for social reasons and dancing became a way to meet new people. French priest, Thoinot Arbeau, assisted this. In his book, entitled *"Orchesographie"* Arbeau described and made popular

Dancing In The Spirit

dances of that day such as the Volta, the Pavane, the Gavotte, and the Allemande to people of different regions. This textbook of dance is still used today as a documentation of the dances of that era.

During this time, special days in the Holy Roman church were celebrated with congregational hymn singing and dancing. Over time, it was said by some critics that the dances began to resemble those done in Greece and Rome in cult worship. As was the fate of all artistic expressions in this era, dance became forbidden. In 744, Pope Zacharias forbade dancing as a part of church worship and fellowship. This tragic time became known as the "Dark Ages" a time when much like the 400-year span between the Old and New Testaments, no communion with God artistic or otherwise was recognized or recorded.

The fourteenth to the sixteenth century marked a Renaissance or 'rebirth' in European history. Artistic expressions began to flourish in Europe and were given a prominent place not only in religious ceremonies but also in society in general. Many monarchs and noblemen began to take an interest in the arts and specifically theatre, music and dance.

The wealthy began to entertain guests in elaborate theatrical displays during balls and banquets. These lavish productions were the predecessors of the ballet, which was actually, first introduced in 1581 by Catherine de Medicis, queen of France. In 1661, King Louis XIV founded the Royal Academy of dance in Paris. Carlo Blasis in Codes of Terpsichore (1825) wrote the rules of classical ballet that are followed still today.

The seventeenth century introduced such dances as the Minuet, the Waltz, and the Polka. The clergy banned the Waltz because it allowed a man to grasp his dance partner's waist. However, the Waltz continued to spread like wildfire even extending itself into the colonies of England on other side of the Atlantic.

In the twentieth century, American jazz came to the forefront of the musical arena and the Charleston became the new dance mania. Modern dance also came into the forefront in the twentieth century. Modern dance moved away from the classical techniques and rigid rules of Ballet. Isadora Duncan became known for what was called free dance. She usually performed in bare feet with loose skirts and draperies.

Ruth St. Denis and Ted Shaw were two other modern dancers who chose not to follow the rules of classical Ballet. Having found inspiration for their dance style in the Middle East, Denis and Shawn formed a school they called Denishawn in 1914. Denishawn produced three of the most well know modern dance performers: Martha Graham, Doris Humphrey and Charles Weidman.

Later during the 1940's, the jitterbug was the most popular dance of the day. The 1940's also brought a wave of movie musicals in which dancers became American national stars. During this era such dancers as Gene Kelly, Fred Astaire and Ginger Rogers were the premiere dancers. The movie musicals were known for elaborate choreography, sometimes classical ballet rules were adhered to and more often tap and modern dance.

In the time period following World War II choreographers emerged who were on the cutting edge. They followed no particular dance styles or codes. They were willing to try things that had never been dared. Some of these avant-garde artists were Merce Cunningham, Twyla Thorpe, Paul Taylor and Alvin Ailey. These dance giants certainly merit more than a simple mention. I would propose that you take the time to read the biographies or at least check your local libraries for videos of some of their performances and choreography.

Dancing In The Spirit

I recognized Martha Graham as a kindred spirit when I read her famous quote, "Dance is the hidden language of the soul." This is so evident in praise and worship dance. The passion for God that is hidden in the recesses of your soul bursts forth and blesses an onlooker in a language that transcends words.

The seventies brought a renewed interest in the classical ballet style and rules. Ballet companies danced before record audiences. The eighties brought a new style of popular dance centered on the emergence of rap music. In this dance style known as break dancing, one of the most complicated and common movements included spinning on the floor on the dancer's back. Break dancing eventually emerged into 'hip hop' dancing, which is associated with the rap music of the nineties and beyond. Rap artists such as M.C. Hammer made hip-hop dancing popular through music videos.

The 1980's also marked a return of the sacred dance. Churches slowly, sometimes skeptically, began to incorporate dance into their worship services. At some churches, dance ministries were formed and were incorporated into the regular devotional time at church services. During the eighties however dancing was not yet accepted by most churches. The nineties brought wider acceptance of dance as a ministry as more churches incorporated dance ministries.

Today it is not uncommon to turn on a Christian television program and see dancers presented as a part of a worship service. However, in most arenas dance is still seen as something 'cute' for the babies to do on 'youth Sunday' or a special presentation that is done for some particular holiday. I am awaiting a time when dance is as integral a part of a worship service as is the singing and the instruments. The call to worship is sounding.....

Karen M. Curry

Dance in Biblical Times

The Bible shows us through many references that the people of God in ancient times were very expressive, using all of their abilities in worship. Dance was a very common expression of praise to God in the Hebrew culture. Dance seemed to accompany most major celebratory feasts and festival. The Hebrew word 'hag' which means dance was interchangeably used in reference to joyous religious occasions.

In Exodus 15:20 when the children of Israel were delivered from Egypt by the opening of the Red Sea, the Prophetess Miriam came forth and led the women in dances and praises before God.

In this the first mention of dance in the Bible, Miriam, the Prophetess is dance leader. She is called here 'Miriam the prophetess, sister of Aaron', although she is also the sister of Moses. She is probably associated with Aaron here because instead of placing her as an equal with Moses, she is placed in association with Aaron, the Priest.

This places dance in a very interesting perspective. First, the dancer (leader) here is not any layperson. She is a prophetess. She is one who communicates God's heart and mind to the people. She is in reality the first congregational praise leader. She tapped into the heart of heaven and pulled onto the earth the praise that was erupting there over their victory in crossing the Red Sea and defeating Pharaoh's army. She is actually leading the congregation into praise, which is the ultimate goal of the worship leader.

Secondly, this passage places Miriam, the dance leader into the prophetic arena as well as into the role of church leadership. If we see Moses in this instance as the modern day senior pastor and Aaron as the presbytery (or associate ministers), Miriam as the modern day worship leader is associated with Aaron. She is recognized as a leader and a prophetess in her own right.

Another reference to dance is made in Luke 15, the parable of the prodigal son. Dance is shown here to be an integral component of the ancient Jewish culture. When the long-lost son returned home, the father, overtaken with joy, commands a celebration to be prepared on the boy's behalf. Later, when the elder son approached the house, the King James Version states that he heard music and dancing. Why would the Bible say that the son *heard* dancing?

There was a celebration. There was music and merry-making. The natural assumption of that time and culture would be that there was dancing. The two in the Jewish culture go hand in hand. There was no separation. Where there was one there was the other.

For instance, in the book of Matthew chapter 11, verse 16, it is written, *"We have piped unto you and you have not danced. We have mourned unto you and you have not lamented."* Although in this verse Jesus is using an analogy, the purpose of an analogy is to use an everyday real life situation to relate a deeper spiritual meaning.

Judging from this parable, it would seem that in this culture, if music were provided, etiquette would dictate that the receiver would dance to show appreciation for it. Not to dance to music provided would be a serious breech of etiquette. The verse relates feelings in the Jewish culture that were considered reasonable and consistent with such an occasion.

The book of Jeremiah also shows us dance as a cultural expression of joy as well as an outward show of peace and exuberance with God's goodness and provision.

> *Again I will build thee, and thou shall be built, O virgin of Israel: thou shalt again be adorned with thy tabrets. and shalt go forth in the dance of them that make merry.*
>
> Jeremiah 31:4

In this passage the Lord, through Jeremiah, promises Israel that He would rebuild her and that she would dance again like the ones who make merry. There are three inferences in this scripture. The first is that Israel was once adorned with tabrets and she in times past danced for joy because of the building and provision of her gracious King. The second inference is that people who make merry do so by dancing.

The third and most important inference is that the Lord preferred Israel when she was dancing as opposed to when she was not. The point is not so much that God loves the dancing but it is the spirit that the dancing represents. Dancing is a natural, expressive outpouring of joy. As asserted in this scripture, God prefers to see this kind of praise and merriment to sour-faced sobriety in praise.

Again, in the same chapter, in the twelfth and thirteenth verses, the Lord, through the Prophet Jeremiah referrers to dance as a natural outpouring of a joyous and grateful heart. The twelfth and thirteenth verses read 'and they shall not sorrow any more at all.' and then 'Then shall the virgin rejoice in the dance...'. So when there is an end of sorrow and grief, and the people of God are happy and satisfied, then dancing will erupt in the temple. We see today a resurgence of the expression of dance in the church universal. It seems that God's people are seeing that if we recognize the finished work of Jesus sorrow and grief have ended. We look forward to the day when the entire body of Christ will join us in the dance.

Dance hang-ups

As we have determined, from the beginning, music and dancing were twins. To separate them is to have half of the picture. However, many 21st Century churches have difficulty accepting dance in the same way that we readily accept music. Dance is a visual art form. It demands attention. Because of its very nature—using the entire body to express. It is very vulnerable to distortion. Because of this what is presented at times is praise that has not yet been quite perfected. All of our own influence has not been sufficiently dissected from the offering therefore we sometimes see so much more of the flesh than the spirit. Thus, it is disappointing, sometimes distracting and markedly lacking of any power to bring life.

Nevertheless, St. John 1:3 declares that 'all things were created by God'. Also Revelations 4:11 reveals that God not only created all things but He created them for His pleasure. Miriam and David danced before the Lord not to mention the ministers that danced before the Lord's presence in David's Tabernacle. We are commanded Psalms 149:3 and 150:4 to praise Him in the dance. So rather than ignore or ban this art form from its rightful place in worship, we can choose instead to submit it to the Holy Spirit for His approval so that it can be a river that ministers life wherever it flows.

Let's examine some of the concepts whether justified or irrational that hinder dance from operating or being seen as a river of life.

Dance Is secular...?

Webster's New World Dictionary defines the word 'secular' as "worldly, not religious". As stated in the previous chapter, from the beginning of recorded history, music and dance have been an intricate part of worship. The earliest recorded dances in secular history were actually performed by priests in religious ceremonies and rituals.

Dance, when it is real dance, is physically expressing the emotions, urges and unctions buried deep within the human soul. If you are a worshipper these expressions are offered to God-whoever you perceive God to be. Let me clarify--there is only one God. However there are worshippers who don't yet know that or cannot yet perceive that because their eyes have not been opened to this truth. Nothing about this art form is secular. Nothing about humans expressing the deepest urges of their souls is non-religious. The scripture tells us that "deep calls to deep". Those deep urges call out to Something or Someone deeper than ourselves.

Unfortunately, now in most current artistic expressions we've failed to go to those deep parts of ourselves. Now the most visible art that we see expresses the superficial urges of a perverted society. Thus, most art has become singularly and markedly perverted whether sexually or otherwise. So we perceive dance as secular because it has moved away from expressing anything of value. The deepest human yearning for love, or expressions of pain or joy or sorrow even anger are absent in the dances that we see most often. However this doesn't change the fact of what dance was created to be. In its purest form it is worship.

Dance is too sensual...?

Another problem that Christians face with the dance is the hesitancy of presenting our bodies in worship. Whether it is for fear of being a sensual distraction or if it is the fear that the body is not perfectly fit enough to be presented, we are somehow hung up in this dilemma.

Of course, we in no way want dance to be a stumbling block. So we endeavor to always present our worship in dance with wisdom and maturity. In addition to endeavoring to present choreography which is true to the heart of the artist's music or to the message that the Holy Spirit is conveying, the choreography must also be conservative. Costumes should be chosen to support the message of the dance as well as to modestly cover and compliment each dancer.

The apostle Paul states that our bodies are holy and acceptable to our Father when presented for His service (Romans 12:1). And David declares in the Old Testament that we are fearfully and wonderfully made (Psalms 139:4)! There's no reason to fear dance that is presented tastefully and prepared by someone who is trustworthy and mature. To ban music or dance from our praise and worship expressions is to 'throw out the baby with the bath-water.' The fear that these expressions may be presented in error or may cause another to stumble cannot outweigh the command in Psalms 149 and 150 to praise God in music, on the instruments, and in the dance.

God loves our praise in all of its forms and to this end let's prayerfully allow the Holy Spirit to refine and shape our offerings into a form that will not only minister life but will also please and touch His heart.

Window-watchers and other Critics

In II Samuel 6 King David has made a prayerful decision to go and retrieve a precious artifact of his culture from Kirjath-jearim, a city in Judah, and bring it into the City of David. What David was to retrieve was the Ark of the Covenant. This was the Ark that Moses was commanded by God to build in Exodus 25. Everything in the Old Testament is a symbol of the New Testament and the Ark of the Covenant is no exception. Although this Ark is a picture of God's Covenant with man, it symbolizes much more. Physically it was a box much like a chest measuring about 5x3x3. It was made of incorruptible acacia wood which symbolizes the human spirit and overlaid inside and without with gold representing divinity. This Ark is a symbol of the covenant dwelling place of God; humanity covered with God's divinity. It can also be said that it is a symbol of Jesus his humanity and deity dwelling in one.

The lid of the chest had two cherubim made of beaten gold kneeling on either side facing one another. The wings of the cherubim were outstretched so that they formed a seat in the middle called the Mercy Seat. A brilliant light, which was known to be God's Shekinah Glory, dwelt between the cherubim. This Mercy Seat is significant in many ways the first of which is that God promised Moses that He would meet him there between the cherubim (Exodus 25:22).

The Ark held the original tablet upon which the finger of God wrote the Ten Commandments. This is a symbol that speaks of the Law of God written inside of man's heart—again pointing to the new covenant. It also contained Aaron's rod that budded (Numbers 17). The inclusion of his rod in the Ark symbolizes God's justification of Aaron after being rejected as High Priest. In this Aaron is a type of Christ, the rejected High Priest justified by God himself. It can also be seen as a type of the resurrection, a branch separated from the tree that not only budded but also even in death produced fruit. The last element in the Ark was a golden pot of manna. This was the same manna that God provided for the Children of Israel in the wilderness. This of course also symbolizes Jesus as the Bread of Life. So ultimately, the Ark of the Covenant uses Old Testament symbols to point to Jesus who is the cornerstone of the New Covenant.

Understandably, it was a great desire for David to be able to go and retrieve the Ark and to be able to return it to the people of God and keep it in his kingdom. However, in his zeal to have the Ark, he failed to consult the instructions. In Num. 4:15, Deut. 31:9, I Chron. 15:2, 15, Ex. 25:14 God gave specific commands concerning the Ark. It was never to be touched by man or animal and the penalty for such a breach was death.

Observably, the handling of the sacred instruments was a sacred responsibility. However, God made provision for this responsibility and made this provision known in the Law.

> But thou shalt appoint the **Levites** over the tabernacle of testimony, and over all the vessels thereof, and over all things that [belong] to it: they

Dancing In The Spirit

shall bear the tabernacle, and all the vessels thereof; and they shall minister unto it, and shall encamp round about the tabernacle.

Num 1:50

The Children of Israel consisted of 12 tribes each being of the lineage of one of Israel's 12 sons. The tribe who were the descendants of Levi were called by God to be priests. The Levites were given to Aaron and his sons to help serve in the temple. The Levites served many functions in the temple (see page 72). Numbers 4:4 tells us that there was a family of the priests called the Kohathites who were specially educated and trained to care for the tabernacle and the things of the tabernacle. Numbers 4:15&20 New International Version states:

> vv. 15> After Aaron and his sons had finished covering the holy furnishings and all the holy articles, and when the camp is ready to move, the Kohathites are to come and do the carrying. But they must not touch the holy things or they will die....
>
> vv. 20> But the Kohathites must not go in to look at the holy things, not even for a moment or they will die.

God made provision so that the Kohathites did not have to touch or see the holy things in order to perform their duties. The Ark specifically was fashioned with golden rings attached to the bottom of it. Long golden poles could be inserted through the rings and the Kohathites would place the poles upon their shoulders to carry the Ark.

In David's sincere zeal to bring the holiest of all the artifacts to his home he made one grave error. David commissioned the singers and the musicians of the House of Israel and gathered together Israel's thirty thousand chosen men. Can you see this stately procession? Israel's best--the 30,000 chosen men, the royal orchestra, only the finest singers, and of course the King, decked out in his finest leading the procession. If David were anything like us, I would imagine that the King was being borne on the shoulders of his servants while the presence of God was being carried on *an ox cart*!

Everything seemed to go well as the royal procession reached the threshing floor at the edge of town. I can imagine David's eagerness to have his God's presence abiding in His Kingdom.

Suddenly one of the oxen stumbles. A panic rises in David's chest. Thank God Uzzah, the Kohathite, reached out to keep the Ark from falling. Wait a minute! Uzzah has fallen! The procession halts and waits for Uzzah to recover. David leans over to his first man "Please remind me that I must properly reward Uzzah for being so quick with his hands. It would be a disaster to have the Ark fall in transport."

"Of course your majesty" the aide answers and scribbles a quick note to himself. There is a pregnant pause. Uzzah is still not moving. One of the other servants stoops to check on Uzzah, he looks up, some words a passed..... someone else stoops.....

David anxious to get the procession moving again leans impatiently over to the aide "Daniel, go and see what is keeping them. I want the Ark in the Kingdom before the fall of night."

"Yes your majesty."

David stands and impatiently checks the slant of the shadows on the ground. Glancing at the sun he mumbles something about losing precious daylight. David lights from the chariot as his top aide approaches.

"Well out with it man, what is the problem!"

"Excellency," belatedly King David notices the pale look on the face of his servant, "It would seem that Uzzah ---"

"Yes, Uzzah—" David prompted.

"Sir it would seem that Uzzah—is—is d-dead."

The King stares dumbly for a long moment. "Dead? But that can't be."

The name Uzzah means '*human strength*'. Uzzah in this passage represents the flesh. Strength is indicative of the striving of human flesh to so something that God commanded to be done by the Spirit. This is the mistake that David made in transporting the Ark of the Covenant. He, being ignorant of God's law, did by the flesh what proved to be fatal for one of his men. The scriptures read that God's anger was kindled and he smote Uzzah (II Samuel 6:7).

Dr. R.C. Sproul in his book '*The Holiness of God*' makes the point that Uzzah assumed that his hand was less polluted than the ground. "But it wasn't the ground or the mud that would desecrate the ark it was the touch of man," he further states.

After this incident, King David was discouraged even to the point of being fearful of God. He allowed the Ark of the Covenant to remain at the household of Obededom the Gittite for three months. When David received word that the Ark had blessed the household of Obededom, he was comforted and decided to try again to return it to Israel where it belonged.

This time David took time to consult the law. In fact, King David called together the Levites or the "priests of praise" to cleanse themselves and prepare to carry the Ark upon their shoulders as God had commanded. (I Chronicles 15:12-16)

After the Ark had been borne six uncertain steps on the shoulders of the Kohathites, the King stopped and made a sacrifice to the Lord on the spot. David was so overjoyed that he leapt and danced before the Lord with all of his might.

This is the most noted example of dance in the Bible. David, because of an overwhelming sense of gratitude and joy, releases himself uninhibitedly in praise to God. There is absolutely nothing more that can be done in a physical body when a feeling of complete rapture comes. If we could, we would fly, but since we are limited as humans, we do the next best thing that we can; we dance!

However, even this, being the finest example of uninhibited, spontaneous, exultant praise in the Bible, was not without its critic. Remember Michal, the daughter of Saul who was given to David to wed as a gift for slaying Goliath?

Michal stood craning her neck in the window of the King's palace. The evening breeze was carrying with it the faint sounds of rejoicing. She knew that shortly the King's procession would be arriving back into the Kingdom. "What no dead bodies this time," she murmured to herself sarcastically turning her back to the window and throwing herself upon her bed. Her maids exchanged a knowing glance. Once again she was in an extremely foul humor.

No one can really understand this temperamental God that her husband served. He was so unpredictable how could David say that he trusted and loved him. "At one time he promised my father and my family that we would rule over this kingdom. And look at it now being ruled by a common shepherd!" She thought bitterly.

As the sounds of rejoicing moved closer into the camp, the maids gravitated to the open window as if drawn by some unseen force. The girlish squeals of the serving women shook Michal from her reverie.

"What is it?' She demanded her arched brows knitting together in a frown.

"Do come and look, your Highness" one of the girls giggled and peeked from behind a kerchief that she was supposed to be mending.

As Michal drew near to the window the girls dispersed waiting for the storm that was surely to come. They watched from a slight distance as Michal gasped and the color drained from her beautiful face. All of a sudden she whirled on them "Leave me!" she commanded imperiously. The girls scattered.

Michal turned back to the window not quite able to believe the sight of a half naked King dancing and frolicking in the street like a common peasant. How dare he! This sort of thing never happened in her Father's reign. This type of emotional, unseemly display would not have been tolerated. Doesn't this backward shepherd know anything about protocol? How could Samuel make such a mistake anointing him be King? "I despise you!" she whispered cruelly as she slammed the windows shut and bided her time waiting for David to arrive.

Michal sprang from the bed as she heard the knob turning on the door. "How are you, wife?" David greeted her brightly.

" I see that you have found your garments."

"Were they lost?" he cast her a confused glance.

"I would hope they were either lost or destroyed seeing as the King was.... how shall I say 'frolicking' without them."

"Out with it, Michal, what is the problem?"

"What is the problem, you ask! David you were out there acting like a raving lunatic and you ask me what the problem is!"

"I was only dancing in praise to my God"

"Well, I guess you didn't know that all of the servant girls were watching and giggling and they weren't thinking one bit about your God! They were watching you perform

for them like the common and vain fellows do. I think you got what you wanted King David. You made a spectacle of yourself and humiliated me in the process!"

In this story, Michal is a picture of the religious, traditional mindset. Judson Cornwall in his study of David wrote the following of Michal:

> *"Michal could see the physical demonstration of David's worship, but she could not see the worship that was in his heart. Those who observe from their palace windows can never understand true worship; they make all judgments from what their eyes can see, they can merely observe actions."*

In many instances, I am sad to say that we as dancers have only given our Michals fuel for their fire. It's obvious why some people have chosen to behave in the example of Michal. If I didn't understand the potential of dance, I might be inclined to agree that it does not belong in our worship services. I have seen so many offerings that were mingled with so much of our own flesh that the focus is no longer God. It ceases from being worship and becomes the blatant display of our own soul's desires and yearnings. Instead of ministering life and instilling a hunger and thirst for God we are unintentionally working counter-productive to the desire of the Holy Spirit.

For instance, costumes are sometimes too sheer -- so much so that bras or underwear are visible. There is nothing wrong with dancing in jeans, shorts, or other street clothes if it is appropriate. Sometimes it is not. Sometimes in an effort to involve our young people, we accept choreography & costumes that do not attribute the focus or attention to God. So we have them involved but are they worshipping? What price are we paying for their involvement? In what are we involving them?

The ministry of dance can be so easily perverted that it is very important that we make sure that what we are offering to the Lord is actually worship. This is why it is essential that the dances come forth originally for the purpose of praise and worship. It is not good enough to pick up something in the world, dust it off and come and offer it to God as praise. I am convinced that people who embrace this second-hand offering mentality aren't totally aware of the awesomeness of the God that we serve.

Enough people with the spirit Michal are simply offended by freedom and liberty. If our choreography and costumes offend them, it is our error. However, if our intentions and motives are pure rest assured that if we consult Him, the Holy Spirit will refine our praise. However, as long as freedom and liberty offend them, it is their issue.

Remember that Michal is a remnant from the house of Saul. She understood the formalities and protocol that were associated with the reign of a king. Notice that when David leads a majestic procession and engaged the royal orchestra and the thirty thousand chosen men of Israel, we hear no complaints from Michal. She very well might have participated with the King in this solemn parade. *"This is the proper way to transport a King and his Queen."* She would have haughtily thought. *"This is the way my father would have done it!"* In other words: To show any emotion, or gratefulness, or passion is not proper. It is not becoming of a King.

Lets consider Michal's life. She had so much to be grateful for. She had lived all of her life as part of the royal family. Her father had been the very first King of God's chosen people. She never wanted for anything. Not only were her needs met, she had the best of everything there was to have. Even when the rest of her family died and her father's lineage was removed from the rule of Israel, she remained as part of the royal family, still had the best of everything, and still resided in the King's palace. Through her womb, her father was given another chance to rule Israel. However, because of her haughty attitude towards the God who had been so good to her, it was not to be. Proverbs 16:5 tells us that every proud heart is an abomination to the Lord. As we read on we find that Michal was barren for the rest of her life.

Michal's judgment mirrors the consequence of people or churches or even denominations that share her haughty attitude. Her empty womb has come to typify the childlessness that is evident in them. Lack of genuine, heart-felt praise transforms what could be a river of living water into a dead pond that emits a foul odor and drives people away instead of drawing them.

When a lack of praise is evident in a church, it becomes just as unproductive as Michal's life. It leaves no legacy, no posterity, no heritage. We see a lack growth both spiritual and numerical and an inability to capture interest especially in young people. Alternately, when a church has a depth of praise and a variety of expressions of praise it cannot be contained inside of four walls. Just as in Ezekiel when the river began to flow from under the temple doors, it could not be contained within. The river ran outside the city and began to bring life to the surrounding areas. This is the prototype. This is our example.

David gave a reply to silence the Michals of our lives. He told Michal, *"It was before the Lord who choose me to rule over Israel, instead of your father, that I danced."* (II Samuel 6:21) In other words, it's okay if you don't understand, I'm not dancing for you, I'm dancing for Him.

If you have a desire to dance, don't let anything or anyone inhibit you. If you feel that you are too heavy, do what you have to to lose the weight. (Trust me, I know the struggle!) If you are not confident because of a lack of training, enroll in classes. If you feel that you are out of shape, try aerobics, running or even walking programs. Do not ignore the gift and calling of God on your life. Realize that you are ushering in the presence of God through your worship. When He sets up His throne in the midst, sickness, disease, poverty, perversion, lusts, and every other hindrance has to bow. The preaching becomes easy, receiving from God becomes almost effortless, the heavens are open, and captives are set free. A river flows from the temple and touches everything in its path with Life. This is the power of your praise!

IV. The Call

Some very common questions that I have encountered about the call to the dance ministry are:

•"Who should dance?"

Whoever feels that they have an interest in doing so. Your interest may well be God-given. Explore it and find out if it is something that God is calling you to do.

•"What size should a dancer be?"

This is a difficult question because no one knows what size Miriam or David were. Afro-Caribbean dancers are usually not the same size as a ballet dancer. Dancer's sizes vary from culture to culture. As long as the choreography is executed with grace and excellence you should be encouraged to dance.

However, if a dancer wishes to be able to perform any dance and to execute any choreography it will be necessary that she/he be physically fit. In other words you should be the optimal size for you--whether that's a size 16 or a size 6. If dance truly is your calling it is your responsibility to make sure that you are physically able to respond to it.

•"What age should a dancer be?"

Again, as long as the dancer is physically able to execute the choreography of the ministry without needing special considerations, they should be able to be a part of the ministry.

If he/she is not able to perform the choreography of the ministry perhaps they should consider choreographing solos at their own level of ability or dancing with young people who are at the same level of ability. It would be wise for the growth and continuation of your dance ministry that someone be identified to work with young people to teach them technique and choreography with excellence. So that as members leave the ministry there will be others trained to take their places. Not to mention that the youths themselves even before they are able to dance with an adult group have the same power resident in their offerings of praise. Expect and accept no less from them.

•"Is formal training necessary to do liturgical dance?"

Formal training is always an advantage. If you can take classes it would greatly enhance your ministry. Formal training adds dimensions of beauty and technique to liturgical dance that can rarely be found without it, however, I would not go as far as to say that it is necessary or a prerequisite. How can anyone say that it is necessary to have taken classes on techniques that were created by man in the 1600's in order to express yourself to God in dance. Dancing to God pre-dates the technique rather than the technique being a prerequisite for it. Who knows but that your dance as original and unprecedented as it may be may inspire a whole new genre of dance? Don't hold back!

If you wish to dance as a career then it is advisable that you take as many classes as you possibly can. It is even a good idea to pursue a degree in this area. However I also suggest that you be open enough to be avant-garde in your dancing. Never cling to technique and training so fiercely that you cannot be open to something that conflicts with it.

•"Is it okay to bring 'street dances' such as 'hip hop' into the church?"

Nothing is wrong with hip-hop style dances. Nothing is wrong with choreography which is up-beat, funky, and hip. However, I would like to caution against problems on two levels.

Again, it may be that your dance, your creativity, and your style may be funkier and more hip than anything you've seen. Please do not allow anyone else to set the trend. Be true to what's in you and don't be a cheap, carbon copy of anyone. Our God is the God who created dance.

My second problem with the idea of dancing street dances in the church is explained by the incident related to us in Leviticus chapter 10 vv. 1-3. Aaron, the High Priest had two sons who were also priests. His sons Nadab and Abihu were trained in the ways of the priests and knew the law well, which gave the 'recipe' for the incense that was to be burnt before the Lords altar.

For whatever reason, Nadab and Abihu decided that they were not going to follow the recipe. They decided that they were going to offer God some common kind of fire. Perhaps this same fire was used for the women to cook by. Perhaps a fire was used to warm the campers at night. Perhaps a fire that was used by the surrounding tribes in their cult worship....who knows? At any rate, God saw it as an offense and the brothers Nadab and Abihu were struck dead before the altar of God.

Moses said to Aaron "This is what the Lord spake *'I will be sanctified among all those who come near unto me, and among all the people I will be glorified'*. In this story, the I believe that the Lord is saying that things that are used for other reasons or things that are created for other purposes are not things that are to be offered to Him.

If you learned a dance to a rap song for the cheerleading squad at school, please don't just reformat it to "Awesome God" and then offer it to God. No! Let's go back to our definition of praise dance. It is dance that from it's origin comes forth with the intent of glorifying God. Make Him a *new* dance. He's worthy.

David once said, "I will not offer to God anything that did not cost me anything." Then how do we offer God dances that did not even cost us the time that it took to create them?

Again, I am not saying that up beat, contemporary style dances are wrong for the church. What I am saying is be assured that your dances are offerings of praise and not a lazy attempt to be so much like the world that you end up offering God, instead of the sweet smell of incense the foul stench of strange fire.

The most frequently asked by new or interested praise dancers is this:

•"How do you know if you are called?"

It's the same as knowing anything else about God. It's faith. God will speak to you in the way necessary to communicate with you and tell you anything that He wants you to know. Don't worry; God knows exactly how to speak to you even if you're not sure you know how to recognize His voice yet. He's your God He knows how to get your attention.

To help you see how easy it is, I will share with you some of the ways that I was able to recognize my calling to this ministry. First, is a genuine interest there? For example, from the time I was a child I was fascinated by dance. While other children my age were out playing I was watching ice-skating, gymnastics, cheerleading competitions, and any other choreographed movement that I could find on TV.

In my teen years, I wanted to be a great dancer. My mother still has a living room with a mirrored wall (isn't God funny!). I would choreograph popular music from the radio in these mirrors as a pastime. While I was supposed to be washing dishes I would play the radio and choreograph in the darkened doors of the broiler oven in the kitchen. Sometimes I still sit in a dark room with the radio on and choreograph songs in my head.

During that, time the TV show "Fame" was very popular. I would watch that show and my heart would

Dancing In The Spirit

burn! I wanted to be in that dance class with Debbie Allen. I wanted to dance in music videos and concerts. I wanted to choreograph like Paula Abdul. But no one I knew who choreographed and danced like that was a Christian. I had never heard of dancing in the church and it never occurred to me that such a thing could be.

I started to choreograph as a cheerleader in junior high school. I continued cheerleading in high school where the sponsor of the squad recognized that I had an ability to not only choreograph and execute the dances but I had a talent for teaching them as well. I was made an unofficial squad teacher. I was the person who was relied upon to teach the new dances and cheers to the girls who had missed a rehearsal. My cheerleading tenure ended when I made a hard decision and took a job in my junior year instead of auditioning. This began a lapse in dancing that lasted until my college years.

When I was a freshman at Florida A&M University (FAMU) there were very few dancing options that appealed to me. I wanted to audition for cheerleading again but some of the suggestive choreography dissuaded me. So I auditioned for a group called the FAMU Connection and did some very minor dancing as well as singing and acting. We followed the travel itinerary of the football team and performed for high school seniors to promote FAMU.

During my sophomore year at Florida A&M my sister invited me to go to church with her. I wasn't that excited about it because through my travels I had begun to stray away from the Lord and I wasn't really in a hurry to make my way back to Him. When we arrived at an overcrowded storefront church, my spirits plummeted. I didn't feel like being in church in the first place and now we had to fight our way through a crowd just to get a seat that I didn't want in the first place!

Before the service got started, at least five people came up and hugged us. That was strike two. I didn't know these people and I certainly didn't want to hug everybody in the church. The service began very promptly. As the first chords of music were played, three dancers made their way to the altar area. My senses perked up immediately.

Every song during the praise service was accompanied by a choreographed dance. The whole church took on an atmosphere of celebration as the musicians played and the dancers danced. They used little props in their hands that they waved while they danced. The congregation responded with little flags that they waved as well. Even though I did not quite understand the scriptural basis for any of it especially the dancing in church, I was very interested and continued to visit the church from time to time.

I joined the church in 1988 and began to grow spiritually and make my way back to God. I attended church every Sunday and my spirit burned as I watched the dancers. I wanted to dance. But I still had my own misgivings concerning dance as it related to church and praise. I couldn't really grasp the purpose of it. It seemed rather trivial to me. It seemed like something that was 'nice' and 'pretty' but not acceptable as praise or worship. And as much as I loved to dance and wanted to accept dance as a part of worship, I just could not see the significance of it as praise or worship. I wanted to dance but more so I wanted to have a real, significant relationship with God. I wanted to touch Him--I wanted to be moved by Him. If this wasn't going to get me there, I didn't want any part of it.

In the Old Testament, the priests would offer animal sacrifices to the Lord. The only way to know if the sacrifice was pleasing was to wait for God to answer the priest's sacrifice with the fire from heaven. Doing something *cute* or *pretty* wasn't enough. I wanted to know that my sacrifice was being accepted. I wanted the fire from heaven to come and consume me in answer to my sacrifice of praise. I wasn't sure that dance could evoke that kind of response from God.

One Sunday morning as I was sitting in church, a woman came to the altar in response to an altar call. She had an illness and some of the elders were praying for her. Quietly, reverently a dancer moved down the center aisle. As she began to dance it was to me as if a holy hush stilled the room. Suddenly, the woman was slain in the spirit. A sense of awe struck me like a sledgehammer. It was beyond comprehension to me that God would grant that kind of anointing to be administered to one in need through a dance. My mind was opened to understand that there was power and significance in this praise. From that point on, I knew that I was called to minister to the Lord in dance. I was ready to accept the call.

Before bed that evening, still struck by what I had seen that morning, I began to pray. I knew that I wanted to dance as ministry because now I understood it's potential. I whispered to the Lord with conviction that night "Lord, I want to dance for You. -- And I want a double portion of the anointing that I saw today."

Doubts Will Come

As time went by, I again began to question the idea of being called to dance. There was no scriptural reference to anyone being called to dance so how could I really say that God had called me to dance. As I continued to study the scriptures, I realized that there was no scriptural reference to anyone being called to sing either; however the music ministry is accepted as a viable calling.

One scripture cleared all of the confusion to me. In John 4:23 when Jesus was talking to the woman at the well, He said 'The *hour cometh and now is when the true worshippers shall worship the Father in spirit and in truth: for the Father seeketh such to worship Him.* ' He didn't say that the Father seeks singers, dancers, musicians, or any specific type of worship. He said that the Father seeks worshippers. I realize now that dancing is one of my gifts, but I am called to be a worshipper. As I continue to meet more and more worshippers, I have learned that many worshippers have several gifts. Many singers also dance; many dancers also sing and play instruments or write. But the calling is to worship.

This scripture relates that as worshippers in spirit and in truth, the Father Himself seeks after us. If someone is seeking you, they call your house or call your name. This is the essence of a calling: God seeking you. If you are a worshipper, Jesus has already said in John 4:23, that the Father is seeking you. You are called. In order to answer the call, begin to seek the Lord. Study the scriptures; spend quiet times of private prayer with Him. Learn His voice. Learn how to invoke His Presence all by yourself. Allow the Holy Spirit to teach you how to conduct yourself in His Presence. But keep in mind that worshippers seek <u>Him</u>— not the anointing, not blessings, not validation. Seek Him. He has to be the focus, the goal, the prize.

Some time later while serving as a dance leader of a local fellowship, I was coordinating a dance workshop where I was to do my very first teaching on the ministry of dance. I was still a little unsure of dance as a bona-fide ministry. Someone whom I respected greatly had recently told me that dance was not a ministry and that it was not anointed. This person felt that only the music that was danced to was anointed. Although I had seen dancers dance with no music at all, somehow, I allowed this opinion to discount all that I had seen and experienced.

I was not comfortable doing a workshop and teaching on dance as a ministry if I wasn't totally sure that it was even anointed. But I did feel that the workshop was necessary because this was to be the first dance ministry at a church where dance was completely new. I wanted to make sure that the congregation as well as the new dancers had an understanding of what dance was and where it belonged in the church. How could the congregation and the dancers understand if I, the dance leader was unsure?

So I began to pray. About two days before the conference, the Holy Spirit said: *'Stop worrying about whether or not dance is anointed. The question is 'Is my life anointed?'"*

God does not anoint art forms, He anoints lives.

This concept can be very tricky for us. Why? Because when we think of the anointing and who 'should be anointed'. We judge by actions. God judges by hearts. Life flows from your heart not from your actions. (Prov 4:23) Sometimes your actions your past and your issues can be in total opposition to your heart. Like the Apostle Paul expressed "I can't seem to do the things that I long to do". But can anyone deny that the author of half the Bible was an anointed man of God?

Furthermore, people who love God and people who are simply religious have many of the same outer actions. However, the scriptures tell us that the Word is the discerner of the thoughts and intents of the heart. Therefore sometimes the ones who by our judgment seem to be the prime candidate for the anointing are at times operating in very little of it. It is essential that we leave this business of judging to God! The following example tells us why....

An Acceptable Offering

Our study of worship would be incomplete without the mention of the most beautiful act of worship contained in the scriptures. Three of the gospels record the account of a sinner woman that dared come to Simon, a Pharisee's house where Jesus was dining. As Jesus was reclining on the floor, eating in the tradition of the time, she stood behind him at his feet and began to anoint him with a costly, precious ointment. In her lovely act of worship, she kissed his feet anointing him with tears and the precious ointment and dried his feet with her hair. The Pharisees and others around whispered about the 'kind' of woman she was. We are not told what her offenses were only that she was a sinner.

The men around knew her past (in other words her actions). They pondered as to why Jesus would even allow her to touch Him. But they didn't understand that it wasn't about her past, her actions, or her mistakes, it was about her tender, broken heart and its desperate desire to touch Jesus. She was broken and humble--fully aware that she was unworthy she risked their disdain and their ridicule just to take that which was most valuable in her life and pour it on His feet. She risked shame and disdain in hopes that she might touch His feet.

The Pharisees who stand by criticizing your worship have no earthly way to judge where your offerings of praise issue from. Only the One who resides within your heart can see the origin of the issues that flow forth. That's why so many times we are dumbfounded when pure, anointed praise flows from vessels that we in our self-righteousness deem unworthy. Yet, when that overflow touches another life, regardless of sins of the past present and future, it explodes into a full manifestation of God's glory and power. Its because of the heart. God draws near to a humble, broken heart. The form of worship is irrelevant—it's the heart that matters.

Jesus heard their whispers and tells a parable to paint a picture of her worship. In His parable, Jesus relays to the men with him that those who are forgiven much love much. If we don't recognize our own sin, don't realize how much forgiveness and grace we've received and are not broken as a result of our own inept attempts to follow the law, we can't really worship nor can we receive the full anointing it takes to minister to others.

In order to worship as God requires it is necessary that we get a proper perspective on who we are and who Jesus is. It is absolutely essential that we, like the elders in John's revelation, cast down our golden crowns at his feet when we worship.

Notice that crowns encircle our heads or our minds. It alludes to thoughts and imaginations. Our golden crowns represent all of our accomplishments, our ideas of who we are and of what we are worthy. However, truth is that the only thing we are worthy of is death. It is only because of the One that we adore that we escaped death.

Second Corinthians 10:5 encourages us to cast down thoughts that exalt themselves against the knowledge of God. This is exactly what the elders did in worship in Revelation 4:10. Although He crowns them with the honor, they remembering His crown of thorns, refuse the honor casting it to the ground before the throne.

This woman did not have a crown of glory, however in I Corinthians the Apostle Paul tells us that a woman's hair is given to her for her glory. As this woman knelt worshipping Jesus, she took the only crown that she had which was her hair and used it as a towel to dry his feet. She realized that which was given to her for glory; that which crowned her was only good enough for his feet. True worship never forgets who we are and who He is.

This woman, believed by some to be Mary Magdalene, offered pure worship that was bathed with her tears. Her worship *moved* her. It came from deep within her soul. It wasn't just a practiced ritual or a rote recitation. It was a deeply heartfelt sincere act of love and adoration. God doesn't want empty meaningless ritual or rote recitations. How do we know this?

Before God will reject an offering, because He is a just God, there has to be a description of the acceptable sacrifice. Just as in Genesis when God had no respect for Cain's offering, it stands to reason that the acceptable sacrifice was explained beforehand, else how would Abel know what to give? For us, Jesus sets the requirements for worship in John 4:24. Those who worship the Father must worship Him in *spirit* and in *truth*.

Truth shows us who we are and of what we are worthy. Many times the only way we reach a place of truth is through trials and errors and falling short over and over again. Once we realize that we are hopeless and destitute without Him, worship is no longer installments on Lake of Fire insurance, or payments on our dues to the 'Bless Me' Club. Worship becomes intimacy—passionate heartfelt adoration. Worship that is devoid of truth and reduced to rote rituals and practiced ceremonies is insulting to God.

Many times, we participate in these rituals out of obligation or in order to appease God so that He'll give us what we want. As though we could really use 10-cent psychology to manipulate an almighty, omniscient God! Hebrews 10 tells us that all things are manifest in the eyes of the One with whom we have to do. Our faulty motives and intents are shouted in the heavenlies and our worship is distasteful. Trading worship for gain takes the intimacy away and makes it currency. Instead of the Bride of Christ, we become like whores—bartering for things the act that should be intimacy.

Love is not real love unless the person loving you is doing it because they see something in you that moves them -- something that caresses their heart. There should exist an unction that is independent of any fear, coercion, threat, or duty. True love doesn't love because it feels it has to. They do not truly love you until they have committed to you beyond feelings and desire. Feelings come and go and desire can be multi-directional. Instead, true love is about who you are that no one else can be. This is the way of worship in spirit and in truth.

Remember perfect actions do not always equal perfect heart. Also perfect heart does not always equal perfect actions. In other words, we can think in prideful error that our meticulous perfection in walking in God's ways is evident of a perfect heart—recognize that as a form of self-righteousness. You see, this means that you are attempting to <u>earn</u> the anointing on your life. Don't be deceived. You cannot <u>earn</u> anything from God. All things from God are received by grace through faith—not by works that any man should boast. (Eph 2:9) It's not righteousness that will 'earn' an anointing. One of the quickest ways to disqualify us from the anointing is to attempt to earn it. You must realize that your total dependence on Christ's sacrifice as a means to right standing with God is essential.

Yes, it is advisable to do everything that you know to do to walk in God's ways—He honors that. But if you did everything in the law and never transgressed against it, it still doesn't give you a perfect heart. Only humbly accepting Jesus' sacrifice and relying upon it and only it for your access to the Father will start you towards a perfect heart. Fasting, prayer, tithing and private communion are excellent and absolutely fundamental to our faith, each necessary in its place and in its proper understanding. However, they are not to be used as cleansing agents, only Jesus' blood can make us righteous. Our works are like filthy menstrous cloths—polluted and dirty.

God never said that he was seeking perfect people. We know David was a man and a worshipper after God's own heart. God's desire to rebuild his tabernacle tells us that. However, who in the scriptures made so many mistakes as David did? And Miriam our other example, after her glorious praise at the crossing of the Red Sea later leads a small insurrection against Moses and is judged by being struck with leprosy. If your heart is after God and your worship is in spirit and in truth God can work with your flaws just as He did David's and Miriam's. The key is to be aware of them accept them and surrender to Him as He begins to work in your life to correct them. This is the beginning of your pursuit of Him.

Notice that the *beginning* of your pursuit is brokenness, humility, truth and total dependence on Jesus' sacrifice. That seems like a pursuit in and of itself but its just the beginning. But be encouraged! He is the author and finisher of our faith. He has begun a good work in us and will complete it. It is working in us both to will and to do His good pleasure. And most comforting, it is Jesus' exceeding great joy to present you faultless before the Father! Just surrender to Truth, He's faithful to do it!

Even if you are not perfect, you are still called. Even if you have totally messed up, you are still called. Even if you don't 'feel' like a worshipper, you are still called. The gifts and callings of God are without repentance. (Romans 11:29) Can you hear it? The call to worship is sounding. The Tabernacle of David is being restored. Can you hear the call? Of course, you can, it is resounding in the heart of the worshipers. This is your call.

The Elisha Principle

Had I realized what a double portion was or how much tenacity, determination, sacrifice and pain (*yes pain*!) it takes to get it, perhaps I would not have spoken so recklessly. Although the anointing is a gift from God freely given at God's own discretion, <u>it is not cheap</u>. Although there is no formula for it, there are principles for it outlined in the scriptures.

In First and Second Kings God gives us some principles of the double anointing. One of the most important principles is that the anointing is *caught* and not *taught*. In other words, in order to receive an anointing you must associate yourself with a person who already operates in it. Not only do you need to associate yourself but also, if you want a *double* portion of the anointing on their life, you need to be humble enough to submit yourself to their leadership. Humble yourself and learn by example. Do whatever you can find to do to promote and better the service of this individual. Make yourself available to God and to the man/woman to whom God has joined you. And, by all means, *be quiet*!

There is much that you can learn from this person; she/he knows enough to have the anointing that you want! Listen as he shows you how he got it not necessarily with words but by example. In the book "God's Armorbearer", author Terry Nance says this:

> You and I will never flow in the anointing of an Elisha until we have learned to serve an Elijah. Jesus said, **Greater love hath no man than this that a man lay down his life for his friends.** (John 15:13). It is not difficult to claim that we are submitted to Jesus but the question is: are we submitted to another human being? That is a different story.

For illustration, let's look at the story of Elijah and Elijah in I & II Kings:

"Lord, there must be more to life than this!" Elisha thought as he stretched the knotted muscles along his back and ran his arm along his sweat soaked brow. His sense of consequence had been deeply wounded by the toil and labor he endured in working his father's land.

Elisha had learned to commune with God during these times of solitude. He knew from the time that he was a small boy that he was called of God to do great things. During times like this, with his faith seriously wounded, he drove himself deeper into his work and meditated upon the writings of Moses and the prophets. Sometimes he replayed the memory of a vision that God had given him time and time again:

An older man comes riding on a chariot into Elisha's village. The man would immediately recognize the calling of God upon Elisha's life. He would explain to Elisha's father that Elisha was meant to be a great prophet and that he must immediately be taken from the fields and taken to Jerusalem to be trained for the ministry. The man would take Elisha on his chariot to Jerusalem and the High Priest would teach him how to be a man of God and minister to God's people.

As Elisha walked with the man, he would show him great wonders and miracles and Elisha would learn to move in the same faith and power. When the man retired from the ministry, he would gently place his mantle upon Elisha's shoulders in the presence of all the great leaders of the Jewish people in a huge ceremony in Jerusalem. His entire village would also be present. He would announce to all that he had found Elisha worthy to be his successor. Elisha would then be placed in a position of prominence in Jerusalem in the temple. And Elisha would receive a double portion of the anointing under which the older prophet served.

But he had this vision since he was a lad and now he was a man. Still had not come to pass. But there was still time.... wasn't there? Of course there was! After all, Abraham and Moses were both much older than he when they were called of God.... weren't they? Oh, blast it all.... Elisha focused his mind upon his work.

He was soon distracted by the figure of a lone man approaching him as he traveled on the path ran along the property boundary. Not many traveled this road and especially not alone. Any of Elijah's countrymen would understand the threat of highwaymen in this area -- he had to be a foreigner. Perhaps the man was looking for lodging. Well, if he needs something let him ask, Elisha thought wearily, I have too much work to do to offer to drive a foreigner all the way back to my father's house. He bent to attend to plowing his father's field again.

He continued to work purposely attempting to clear his mind again. Suddenly he felt the weight of a cloth drop over his head and darkness descended upon him. He pulled the oxen to a halt and pulled the blanket... no not a blanket... a mantle why would this old fool throw his mantle upon him like he was some.... a mantle?! Could it be... was it possible? He looked up and saw that the man was still making his way down the road. "No! No Elisha of course not don't be foolish!" he castigated himself aloud. But just maybe... Elisha left the oxen and ran after the old man. His certainty grew with every step.

"Let me, I pray thee kiss my father and my mother," Elisha panted breathlessly with excitement and exertion, "and then I will follow thee!"

"Go back again, " the old man replied, "for what have I done unto thee?"

Elisha was not willing to take no for an answer. He would not give up the chance of his anointing. He threw caution to the wind. Running back to the field, he unyoked the oxen and slew them. His father's men dropped their plowshares and stared at him in awe. Having gone to far to stop now, he prepared the oxen served them to the people. That is the beginning of the story.

The Bible lets us know that he then followed Elijah and that he *'ministered to him.'* The word minister can be translated as *'to serve.'* Elisha served the older man to such a degree that other prophets knew Elijah as his master. Not only did he serve Elijah but also he watched and observed all that he did. He was with him when he called the fire down from heaven and consumed the Jezebel's men; he was with him when he prophesied Ahab's demise, and through numerous other events in his life. He got a ringside seat to see the miracles of God and his faith was built tremendously. He learned the skill of a prophet from his master. He caught the anointing.

Something else about this account of Elijah and Elisha caught my attention. In I Kings chapter nineteen when Elijah found Elisha plowing the field and he threw his mantle upon him, when Elisha responded by running after him Elijah answered *"Go back again for what have I done to thee?"* At this point, many of us would have been offended and would have gone back and continued plowing. For those who would have turned around it is safe to assume that we probably would have been plowing for a very long time.

I almost allowed myself to become a permanent plower. I almost allowed my hurt feelings to cheat me out of a double portion. It seemed that every other dancer, except me, had some kind of special relationship with the dance leader. They shared things and talked and she listened and laughed and gave advice. There was never any special relationship between us and this made my attempts to serve her feel very awkward. I would complain to the Lord that we weren't friends.

At one point the Lord spoke to me and said "I didn't call you to be friends, I called you to serve her!" Regardless of whether I felt comfortable with her or not, it didn't change the principle of God: if I served her and learned from her I could receive a double portion of her anointing. Even if she didn't like me, it's not up to her, the decision is God's.

Elisha, determined to be blessed, went back and slew the oxen and served them to the people nearby. He didn't care that Elijah had told him in no uncertain terms to get lost. It didn't matter if Elijah liked him or not. He wanted something from God not Elijah.

Even to the end of their relationship, Elisha kept his goal in mind. In spite of continued rejection, on the day that he knew that the Lord would take up Elijah into heaven, Elisha refused to leave his side. In II Kings 2:1 when the Lord would take Elijah up to heaven by a whirlwind, Elijah tried to leave Elisha in Gilgal. However Elisha refused to be left he answered *him 'As the Lord lives and as thy soul lives, I will not leave thee.'* So they journeyed together to Bethel.

Again, in verse four Elijah says to Elisha, *'stay here I pray thee for the Lord has sent me to Jericho.'* Elisha's answer was the same.

Again in verse six Elijah tries to ease away from the younger prophet. Elisha was firm in his decision. His response again was the same. No matter how many times Elijah tried to get away from Elisha, no matter how rejected or offended he may have felt he kept his eyes on the goal that was set before him. He wanted that double portion!

Elisha was faithful to fulfill his call even to the end. Verse eleven reads:

> *And it came to pass, as they still went on, and talked, that, behold, there appeared a chariot of fire, and horses of fire, and parted them both asunder; and Elijah went up by a whirl wind into heaven.*

Elisha was so intent upon not leaving Elijah that God sent a chariot of fire to part them! Regardless of rejection, opposition, or whatever else the enemy might send to try to distract us from our goal we ought to be as steadfast as Elisha. Don't let anything separate you from your calling, your purpose and your destiny. Once you find it be as tenacious as a bulldog to see it through.

There will always be challenges and struggles to divert us from our purposes. As you complete one test, another will come at you in another form more difficult than the first. However, we must be as single-minded as Elisha in order to respond to our call. If you are truly a worshipper, you've already realized that there is no life without Him anyway. You have been marked and you can't exist without His Presence. In the words of the Apostle Paul, I reckon that the sufferings of this present time are not to be compared to the glory, which shall be revealed in us. (Romans 8:18)

Hold on, be strong, you are being prepared to answer the call that is sounding in your spirit. The call to the true worshippers is sounding. It is your call.

IV. The Temperament

I thank God for the call to be a worshipper. I have always loved all forms of the arts and I find it thoroughly fulfilling to work in this area. In fact, it doesn't seem to be work at all.

My experiences in the arts have revealed some interesting similarities in the temperaments of artistic people. Remember that both our key dancers of the Bible also were prophetic; Miriam the Prophetess and God's beloved David the Prophet, Priest and King. The prophetic and artistic natures seem to be somehow intertwined even to the point where artistic/prophetic people share the same temperament.

In our unregenerated state we tend to be moody, irritable and temperamental and just a headache to be around. Artistic/Prophetic/Creative people are also prone to depression, competitiveness, jealously, and criticism especially of other performers. We tend to be very perfectionistic and idealistic. When people that we are working with do not live up to these expectations, the resulting temper tantrums are disastrous. I once had a choir director who would throw chalkboard erasers at us! People tend to feel that they have to 'walk on eggshells' not knowing when the next lapse of depression or emotional explosion will erupt.

The lapses of depression can be severe leading even to contemplations of suicide. Recall the prophet Jonah grieving to the point of wanting to die in Jonah 4:8. Also the prophet Elijah wanting to die in I Kings 19:4.

Dancers specifically are known for being very proud, egotistic people. From the term prima ballerina, which actually refers to the premiere female dancer in a dance company, comes the derogatory term 'prima donna' which refers to the common temperament of all performers which is commonly noted to be erratic, self-absorbed, and volatile.

It should seem obvious that in the unregenerated state creative, artistic, prophetic people are not usually happy people. They are very self-centered as a result, when given more praise, adoration and power because of their talent, they can easily become dangerously off balance. Isn't it just like God to require humility, brokenness and total dependence on Jesus from a person with this temperament. There is no other way to see the fullness of the call on our lives without first submitting to truth and breaking the shell of self-centeredness.

Although this is the *natural* temperament of a performer, the Lord is not satisfied with any of us resting in our natural, Adamic nature. He has called us not to be like the first Adam but the second Adam who is Jesus. The performance attitude is a result of self-centeredness. Lets explore the story of the first performer, he too became dangerously self-centered.

Lucifer led the praise and worship in heaven. He was the star musician, the lead soloist, and the worship leader. He had been perfect in his ways from the day that he was created. He was not *an* anointed cherub he was the anointed cherub Ezekiel 28:13-20. God took time with the creation of this angel his covering was made of every precious stone. God lovingly, patiently weaved the musical pipes and instruments into Lucifer's body so that he actually breathed music.

The Prophet Ezekiel goes on to say that iniquity was found in him. (Ex 28:15) Notice, the scriptures do not say that Satan committed some vicious act in the sight of God. It says that iniquity was found in him. The iniquity is the seed of the act. In other words, it was an *attitude* or an *error* in his thought system that caused him to fall. It is wise to be more concerned about the seed than the act. If you can catch and confess your errors in seed form you can avoid a fall. Lucifer was not so fortunate.

Lucifer desired and sought to establish his throne above God's (Isaiah 14:13). He was competing with God for the highest throne and the greatest glory. He wanted the praise that was God's for himself. This is the result of self-centered, self-absorbed attitude in the area of performance.

The applause, the spotlights, the attention, the praise.... If you are self-absorbed, it becomes easy to forget that it is not about you. You are only the chalice that delivers the wine. If the attention and praise swells your heart, be careful, you are sampling wine that was only meant for God. I read somewhere that *'Praise is food for God, and poison for men'*.

The thought that the people are ministered to by you and your talent instead of the anointing and the Life of God that flows from a river deep within you is error. I call this misconceived delusion the **"Its About Me" Mentality**. Lets review some symptoms of the "Its About Me" Mentality and you can diagnose yourself. A performer who has contracted the "Its About Me" Mentality will be constantly aware of the perfection of their performance. He will have the tech crew adjust the lights three or four times in order to capture his best features. The make-up will have to be perfect in order that she look her best. If her hair is not right, she will not dance. They complain because the costume, even though it is appropriate for the presentation, does not accentuate the finer aspects of their figure. I have seen a singer walk off of the stage after 'worshipping the Lord' and literally blast the sound tech because the microphone was not set perfectly and he had to strain his voice in order to be heard.

In this, where is the love of Christ? Where are the fruit of the spirit? It doesn't matter who we are or what our position in the church is, if we have the singing voice of angels, and the agility and flexibility of a gymnast, if we have the dramatic ability of an academy award winning actor, and have not charity, we are but a tinkling brass and a clinging cymbal. Ministry will be hallow and empty--*ichabod*--void of the presence of God – and powerless to impart Life. The ministry will have no ministry in it. It will be reduced to the menial status of entertainment. *Performance without the anointing is entertainment.*

Standing opposite of the "Its About Me" Mentality is the true worshipper. Using David and Miriam as our examples lets examine this. Miriam wasn't content to praise God by herself at the crossing of the Red Sea. She encouraged the other women to join in and dance before the Lord. In addition, how many times in the Psalms does David command: "Praise the Lord." "O magnify the Lord with me, let us exalt His name together." "You who fear the Lord, praise Him!" Neither was David content to allow the Ark of the Covenant to enter into the City of David without celebration. Even though he was the King of Israel, he allowed himself to be an example of worship and adoration as he danced with all his strength before the Lord. I can see David casting down his golden crown as he totally forgot decorum, protocol and position. After the Ark of the Covenant was restored to the City of David, he appointed worshippers to stand in the temple and minister before the Lord's presence 24 hours a day.

The heart of a true worshipper is in love with God. What fuels their 'performance' is a heartfelt, sincere passion for God and a desire to touch His heart with every move they make. Whether you dances in street clothes or a tutu, the performance is the same. The make-up and hair are irrelevant because when you worship God from your spirit, they will be rearranged by the time the dance is over. Whether there is the proper lighting or sound system or there is not, it doesn't matter. God is guest of honor. Judson Corwall, the noted author of *Worship as David Lived It* says:

"Love that releases all of the heart's adoration, that expresses all of the soul's attitudes, that explains all of the mind's determination, and utilizes all the strength of the worshipper's body is worship. This measure of worship requires a heart that is absolutely fascinated with God….A hungry heart that has fallen in love with God will be a worshipping heart."

The true worshipper's aim is to inspire everyone in the congregation to enter into the ecstasy of worship that he has found. She is not content or even moved by applause. If the only response is applause then she may feel as though they have missed it somewhere. Unless, the congregation is ushered into the presence of God and are worshipping God it wasn't successful.

The identifying factors of a worshipper are these: When they dance there will be no distractions, the congregation will be directed to God. The focus will be on God, the dancer will not be gauging responses or 'playing to the crowd' throughout the performance, it will be as if they're lost in the pursuit to touch God's heart. Third, and most important, the anointing, God's Presence, and His burden-lifting, yoke-destroying power will be manifested. The "All About Me" Mentality has been broken like Mary's alabaster box. The sweet ointment that flows out is a river of living water bringing life to those around it.

The Measure of a Worshipper

The gifts and callings of God are given without repentance. (Romans 11:29) From the time you are in your mother's womb God has called you and in order to help you accomplish your call He deposited inside you gifts and talents. The measure of Godliness in your life is not the measure of your talent—the talent is there before we are aware of God—while we are yet in sin.

In fact, many ungodly people are replete with talent. We should not make the mistake of feeling that because our gift is excellent that means we are more 'godly' than others. The measure of Godliness in our lives is the amount of the fruit of the spirit that is evident in our life—not success, not material things, not loyal supporters or fans, not even record/book/or video sales. There is no other gauge of God likeness.

Just as surely as spiritual death occurred as a result of eating from the tree of the knowledge of good and evil, so a ministry will die without the love of God and integrity of character manifested by the fruit of the Spirit inherent in it.

Remember Lucifer? For His error in thinking, God's prized praiser, the anointed cherub was cast to the ground (Isaiah 14:12). In the New Testament Luke 10:18 Jesus relates to the disciples that he beheld Satan falling to the ground as lightning.

In the same way that God meticulously created Lucifer specifically for music, He meticulously created you for dance. He's been anticipating your arrival for generations. He organized time and nature and even your mother & father's wills in order to bring you about for this season. He orchestrated all the situations and circumstances in your life that crushed your dance out of you like a crushed olive giving pure oil. He has been working in you for years in order that you might be just who you are right now. He has a vested interest. He will finish the work.

However, in the same way that He would not tolerate pride and haughtiness from his beloved cherub, He will not tolerate it from us--His beloved sons and daughters. In the same way that Lucifer, once the anointed cherub, fell from his position, so can we. Notice that Lucifer did not lose his *talent* only his closeness to God and his ability to operate in his talent with the power of God resident in it. (Which we call the anointing) Lucifer's talent no longer

Dancing In The Spirit

brings life and rather than bringing freedom and liberty, it now causes bondage and ultimately death.

When I first began to dance, I was very confident in my ability. My youth and my sometimes-haughty attitude caused me to clash with other dancers. I felt as though my ideas and talent were excellent. Sometimes, they were but what I failed to see was that this talent and my ideas were only in seed form. I needed my leadership first to help me become anointed. I also needed my brothers and sisters to help sharpen me and my experiences with them to crush it out of me in purity

Because He is a good God and committed to finishing the work He started in me, instead allowing me to fall, God allowed me to go through a series of situations where I was being broken over and over again. I found that although my talent was wonderful and recognized by my leaders, it was my attitude that was constantly getting me into trouble.

I learned that what made me an exceptional dancer was His gift. I realized that I would become an anointed dancer as I did what it took to cultivate the anointing on my life. I found that there are scores of talented people in the world. I have met and continue to meet secular and Christian dancers who could dance circles around me. Talent is cheap! Everyone has some talent and most people have a few. However, the anointing is rare and costly.

After enough breaking, I learned to submit to the Spirit of God in my leaders and yes, even in my peers. It was when I was humbled enough to recognize that without God's anointing my talent is useless (entertainment), I began to rely on Him totally. My dancing became a desperate attempt to please Him and to touch His heart. Only then was I able to begin to flow in the anointing and minister life.

Karen M. Curry

In the University of the Holy Ghost where classes are held in the nearest prayer closet, I learned the Elisha Principle. Remember the way to the double anointing is to serve that person as Elisha did or Elijah in I Kings 19:19-21 or as Joshua did Moses (Exodus 24:13) or as David did for Saul in First Kings. This is one way to conquer the "Its About Me" Mentality and truly become a worshipper. It can't be all about you if you acknowledge that someone else is greater than you in your area and you submit yourself to serve them.

After learning this, I set my mind on serving my dance leader. I did whatever I could to serve her. I washed dishes; I helped prepare Sunday dinner; I folded clothes; I did her hair; I did whatever she needed to be done. Not to impress her because promotion doesn't come from man. I did this to work the Elisha Principle in my life. I wanted what she had. I wanted God's anointing.

Notice in II Kings chapter 2, after serving Elijah for the allotted time, Elisha got the double portion that he'd sought. The mantle or coat of the prophet is representative of the power and anointing that rests upon him. As Elijah was being carried away in the whirlwind, his mantle fell to Elisha immediately used it to part the Jordan River as he had seen his master do.

About three years after I determined to be my dance leader's Elisha, I moved from Tallahassee to Orlando. In Orlando, I had the opportunity to teach dancers at several different churches. I also worked as the Director of Dance and Theatre at a local inner-city ministry called Frontline Outreach.

I have had the opportunity to teach special sessions at Schools and recreation centers. I have had groups to dance at parks, shopping malls, and the Orlando Arena. My choreography has been used in debutante balls, parades, and local plays. One of the greatest accomplishments was that I had a group of dancers to do an impromptu performance for former President George Bush.

> A man's gift makes room for him,
> And bringeth him before great men.
>
> Proverbs 18:16

Humility goes against the very nature of the performer because all of us in our unregenerated state have the spirit of the first performer. Just because we do become regenerated doesn't mean that our unregenerated nature disappears like a rabbit in a magic show. We have to consistently make choices and we have to determine to make our flesh submit to the Spirit. We must humble ourselves and wait for God to exalt us (I Peter 5:6).

It is God's goal for us to be as famous as possible. He wants to exalt us. Remember God's first and foremost; purpose is to win the world to Him by His love, which is showcased through us. If you are willing to be a showcase of His love, not just in your presentations but in your life every day then God is willing to use you to fulfill His intent which is to bring them into fellowship with Him in maturity and perfection.

Feed My Sheep...?

When the curtains close and the glare of the spotlight fades, people are drawn to the talented, gifted person of God and the glory that surrounds them. But wait--is that really glory or the glitter of the makeup--the glow of the theatre lights? Are you like the Wonderful Wizard of Oz all special effects and no substance? When they draw near what do you have to offer them? Will your life off stage minister life to them? Jesus said that the words He spoke were spirit and life. That was the same whether he was preaching to a crowd of 5,000 or if He was speaking one on one to a woman caught in adultery.

You might feel like I did, like you have great talent and that God should be using you more than He is. You may even be tempted to take matters into your own hands and create opportunities for yourself. However, until we understand that it's not our talent that God is interested in but more so our lives, He can't trust us to do what He would desire.

God's goal has been the same since the garden. He desires to bring mankind as a whole and as individuals into fellowship and communion with Him in maturity and wholeness. We must come to truly accept and appreciate that our talent is valuable tool to assist in accomplishing that. So in order to understand your talent in its proper perspective, we have to see it in respect to God's plan and use it to accomplish God's plan. Seek first God's purpose and His kingdom. Sincerely allow God to search your heart to be sure that riches and fame are fringe benefits and not the bulls eye. Will you be just as committed if God calls you to minister to those who can't pay you for your gift? What is your first purpose—the fringe benefits or the Kingdom?

When people see anointed people, they want to be around them and talk to them and just get to know them. They are set free by the anointing and drawn by talent. The misconception is to think that this hero-worship that a baby Christian may have for a performer is a testimony to the performer's greatness. Not so, this is a testimony to God's anointing accomplishing its mission and it is an opportunity to disciple.

This is the real test of readiness: Is there enough fruit on your branches to feed and nurture those whom the anointing might draw? In Matthew 21:19 Jesus went to a fig tree looking for fruit. He was hungry and the fig tree had leaves and branches and was presenting itself as though it had what Jesus needed. However, when Jesus approached the fig tree there was no fruit. Jesus cursed the tree. Why? Because if it was not the season for figs why did the tree present the signs that it had figs? It was a fake—a disappointment. All smoke and mirrors—no substance.

This is the same façade we purport when we as worshippers do not have the fruit that a baby Christian needs when he approaches us after the performance. *"But the anointing was there, and it looked like they had what I needed but when I got closer I found nothing."* How disappointing for a hungry world to walk up to our branches and find nothing but leaves. Measure yourself—are you bearing fruit? Or have you allowed the performance, the fringe benefits to become the pursuit? If God is the pursuit and getting to know Him better getting closer to Him there would never be a lack of fruit.

When I first moved to Orlando, I ran here and there from this talent agency to that one trying to find an opportunity. I finally I took a job teaching dance for an after-school program. During this humbling experience, I had to learn that I if I never attained my 'dream' I still loved to praise Him and would continue to do so regardless.

Almost a year later, one of the talent agencies that I had called and totally forgotten about called me and offered me an extra part on a television show. Understand that an extra is a very, very small non-speaking role but I was excited because I saw it as a chance, a beginning. Later I understood that God opened the door for me to allow me to see that my heart had changed. The agency called everyone back for a second day of filming. I turned down the offer and went back to work teaching dance in the after school program.

Later I was offered an administrative position with a large company in Orlando handling entertainment contracts. I turned that position down too. It wasn't the right time in my life. I was questioned for years about those decisions but I had come to know what I live for and where my destiny is headed. Its not about the performance, its about the pursuit. Everything that I choose and everything that I involve myself with has to fit into the pursuit. If it doesn't then it has to be forsaken. My life is the pursuit.

In order to continue with the pursuit, be willing to be in control of your dream rather than letting it control you. Be content to put on your best performance in your prayer closet. Never let the mesmerizing glare of the spotlight cause you to forget your true passion. Fall in love with Him. Pursue Him with your whole heart.

Lets not forget that even as Satan was created as a performer, his primary job was to worship before God. This is what all performers are created to do, to use their talents to minister to God first. I would encourage you therefore, not to see yourself as a performer but as a worshipper to remind you of who you really are. Do not call what you do performing, rather call it ministry and treat is as ministry. You are ministering first to God and the anointing that it creates overflows from your heart to the congregation as rivers of life begin to flow.

During my breaking process, I was dismissed from the dance ministry. I sat on the pew during church services and felt as though I was dying. When I saw the other dancers ministering, I felt jealous and I criticized every mistake they made. I felt as though I was wasting away because I could not express myself to God like I wanted to. But I had a choice, I could go through all of this turmoil for a reason and actually get something from it or I could go through all of it for nothing. I was determined that I would grow in the situation. I wanted to learn from it. I humbled myself and asked God to show me what He wanted me to learn.

The Holy Spirit taught me that when you are a worshipper and you have a desire to worship God, it doesn't matter who sees you worship or who doesn't. It doesn't matter who is blessed by what you're doing, your souls

Dancing In The Spirit

desire is worshipping God with your gift. You want to touch His heart; you want to express your love.

In I Samuel 16 King, Saul was looking for some one to play before him to cause the evil spirit that was plaguing his life to leave. Someone suggested that the King appoint David the son of Jesse, a shepherd. How did one of the King's advisors know of David, the son of a shepherd? Where had David been practicing his skill all these years? He was the son of a shepherd; he had surely never come before any of the King's men to play before.

David was always out in the fields tending the sheep. He spent much time alone and during those times, he learned to minister to the Lord on his harp. I believe that he learned to commune with God during those times. Can you imagine a soldier, perhaps one of the King's friends passing through the pastures on the way to the palace and overhearing the most beautiful harp music he had ever heard. He probably inquired of his men and found that that pasture belonged to Jesse the Shepherd and that his son David was the one who tends the sheep.

David was willing to humble himself to be content caring for the sheep, although he had a beautiful talent for lyric and music writing. He wasn't sending out demo tapes and headshots to local talent agents. He was ministering to his only earthly audience never minding that it was a herd of sheep. God exalted him. It was through his talent that he came before the King. But it was by his anointing that he was exalted into his destiny.

Judson Cornwall says this:

> It seems consistent that the persons who get the 'lucky breaks" are also persons who discipline themselves to use "idle" time to develop their abilities."

During those times when you find you are not operating in your gift for whatever reason, you'll feel like Jeremiah... like fire is shut up in your bones. If you don't release it in worship you will see the ill effects of it. You will become bitter, self-absorbed and eventually discouraged and depressed. You have to release it for your own spiritual health. Even when you feel that there is no outlet, no way to release it, there always is.

During the time when I wasn't dancing in church any longer, I had become depressed and bitter. However, God was teaching me something. During a time of prayer, God challenged me to get dressed in my best dance costume and put on some music and dance before Him as though I was dancing before thousands of people.

From time to time, I still have private recitals for The King. I have found that an audience is necessary in order to perform, but not to worship. If we always keep in mind that we are worshippers, we will only require an audience of One.

Understand that there are exceptionally talented saints that never achieve the destiny that God has planned for them. They are so consumed with the dream that they lose sight of the Dream-Giver. In order to fulfill the purpose that God has created you for as a worshipper you must commit your works to Him and allow Him to establish your thoughts (dreams). If you delight yourself in Him, He will give you the desires of your heart. (Proverbs 16:3, Psalms 37:13&14). You have to be willing to let your dream die--completely--in order to realize it. (John 12:24)

It was only after Jesus' suffering (breaking) and death that he experienced resurrection. Along with resurrection, all power was given to Jesus. How much more so will death be expected of us? After death to the "All About Me" Mentality, death to our pride, death to our 'golden crowns' will we be resurrected with the power of the anointing in our lives. The way to that river that brings life is through the doorway of spiritual death.

VII. The Order

"Let all things be done decently and in order."
I Corinthians 14:40

Leadership Training

All authority is ordained of God. (Romans 13:1) So both the dance ministry and the dance ministry leader must understand that God placed the leader in authority in order that the ministry be run in accordance to the vision that was placed first in the Pastor's heart. In short, your goal is to promote someone else's vision. As a leader in a local body your goal should be promoting and working within the vision of your Pastor and mission of your church. Your job is not only to instruct the dancers in dance but also to promote and be an example of the lifestyle set forth by the vision of the church. The vision of the church should be ultimately based upon the principles set forth in the Bible.

If you happen to be a leader who is working outside of a local body, this is a perfectly acceptable position. However, examine yourself by answering these questions: Am I submitted to a local spiritual authority? Is my local spiritual authority supportive of this outside Dance Ministry? Have I also invested time in the dance ministry of the local church? If one is unsure of any of these things consider whether the example of submission to authority being displayed is one that dancers who will be under your authority should follow.

If a door-to-door salesman came to your door selling computers. Before you invested any money in his product you would want to know what company he represented wouldn't you? You would want to know the company's reputation? He would need some type of credibility in order to convince you to invest, right? What if he told you that these were none of your concern? Your only concern was that he was a good salesman with good products. Would you buy from him? Regardless of how good his sales techniques are or how good his products are, if he has no company behind him, can you trust him?

Well, how much more so with a ministry or calling? Someone promoting themselves as a minister doesn't mean much. The question is: Why they aren't operating under authority? I would want to be assured that someone laid hands and sent them forth. I want to know who their spiritual father is and what his ministry is like. Without knowing such things it's quite likely that this 'minister' could be a renegade from some God-ordained ministry and by joining to him, you too become a renegade. If someone is rebelling against authority, it doesn't matter how many people he can convince to join with him, he is still a rebel. The only thing that will validate such a ministry is repentance and proper submission to God given authority.

Being committed to another person's vision does not mean that you don't have a vision of your own. It simply means that you are wisely choosing to serve someone else's vision faithfully until it becomes time for your vision to be manifested. Habakkuk 2:3 tells us that the vision that God has given you is for a specific appointed time. Then the question becomes what to do in the mean time.

Dr. Michael Landsman, in his book *Supportive Ministries* gives us an answer. He states:

> "It is important that you realize that preparation time is not lost time. Don't be over-anxious and jump out ahead of God. It is a good idea to get involved in another ministry and be faithful in what you do.
>
> " Not every one is called to the frontlines. You may be called to full-time ministry; but until you

get there, you need to be active in a supportive role within the Church. That is were you learn—where you grow."

In Luke 16:12 Jesus asks this question: "And if you have not been faithful in that which is another man's, who shall give you that which is your own?" Selah, as David would say. Pause and think about it.

A Leader's Responsibility

It is the role of leadership to present a living-breathing example of the principles of God. By doing this, we will inevitably inspire those who follow us to strive to do the same. We will also show them that God's principles work and they work right here in your corner of the world, in your community and on your block. There are no excuses—if I can do it you can too.

As a dance leader, one of our responsibilities is to whet the appetite of the entire congregation but especially of those that work closest with you which are the dancers. Through your praise dance, show them a visible demonstration of the pursuit and a desperate longing for God until it is birthed in their own hearts. Once that occurs a more passionate degree of seeking becomes evident in their praise and worship. As it becomes evident in their praise they become examples to the congregation and the hunger is birthed in them too and they begin to praise. If the whole church is praising with a desperate hunger… Can you see it? That river of life flowing from under the doors of the temple! Where did it start? Out of the bellies of the saints of God.

Our dance ministries should be first partaker of the gift and the anointing that God has given to us. We should use those gifts to regularly to demonstrate to them how to create an atmosphere in which God will dwell, how to lift a feeling of heaviness from their own lives, and how to offer sacrifices of praise. We should also during rehearsals and meetings make sure to practice creating an atmosphere that God will inhabit and show them how to conduct themselves in this atmosphere, when to dance, when to be still, how to move at what time, and when the atmosphere lifts—when the anointing is gone, the dance is over.

Have you ever wondered how David got to be a man after God's heart and eventually the greatest King Israel ever had? I think that it had something to do with the time that he spent in the pasture tending the sheep. During this slow season of his life, David learned the leadership principles that would establish and guide him into being the greatest King that ever ruled Israel. He learned praise and worship that spilled forth out of his life with such power that the anointing that it caused King Saul to be delivered from a tormenting spirit. It also demonstrated to Israel their King's great love for God during the transport of the Ark of the Covenant. He learned humility that kept him from leading an insurrection against King Saul. Although he had 400 committed men, David was humble enough to realize that the prophecy of his reign was for an appointed time.

One of the greatest principles of leadership that David learned came from day after day after day of just being a shepherd. He learned how to care for sheep, how to lead them, how to anoint them, how to feed them, how to comfort them. I think that David's knowledge of a shepherd's heart lead him to liken God to the Good Shepherd the 23 Psalms. The parallels drawn here are significant in understanding our roles as leaders.

Notice that the Good Shepherd gives His beloved sheep green pastures to lie in and still waters to drink from. The strange thing about a sheep is that in order for a sheep to lie down, all of their needs have to be met. A good shepherd knows what sheep need and without complaining or belittling them for their needs, he provides it. Do you

Dancing In The Spirit

know what the dance ministry needs? Do you provide it? If there is one that needs extra attention or a little more encouragement, do you provide it? Do you do so without complaining and tearing them down?

The scripture states that the rod and the staff of the Lord, which are representative of his authority and his correction, comfort the sheep. It must be the same with leadership. The people that God has entrusted to us should feel comforted by the fact that we have authority and that we have the ability to correct. In order for someone to be comforted by authority and correction, they must know that it will not be used in a vindictive or biased manner. They must know by experience that the leader's authority and correction are tools that are used or their protection as well as for their betterment.

David goes on to say that the Lord anoints his head with oil. Anointing the sheep's head with oil was a protective measure. It kept away the bugs and flies that drew the precious life-blood out of them. In the same way, we should protect the ministry by lovingly exposing them to the anointing of God regularly to keep away the spirits that plague and destroy their lives. Again, the dance ministry should be first partaker of the gift that the Lord has given to us. If there are broken people, strife, and inner struggles in our dance ministries then how can we prove that there is an anointing that breaks yokes and lifts burdens?

Finally, David says, 'my cup runneth over'. This analogy speaks of prosperity, gladness, joy, and peace. Although we all know that trials and tests and temptations will come as long as we live. And as long as two people who are humans have to work together there will sometimes be disagreements. However, the norm should be a cup that is running over. The problems that come should be temporary and the peace, prosperity, and joy should be the norm.

Rebellion and Consequences

Don't, however, be dismayed when strife and contention is noted among the dancers. That's only natural. God placed the leadership there to deal with these things. These types of problems are solvable. Problems where the followers are striving with a leader are a different thing altogether. Although there is a solution, usually it takes an authority higher than one's self to administer it.

Bucking against authority is ultimately bucking against God. A story in Numbers illustrates this point:

After Israel was miraculously delivered from Pharaoh's army at the Red Sea, the Children of Israel sang and danced joyously before the Lord. Their praise and appreciation was, however, short lived. A short time later in the wilderness, they became disillusioned. They murmured and complained that they had been aimlessly wandering. *"Surely it doesn't take this long to cross a desert!"* They began to question the things that Moses had told them. *"What if there really wasn't a God up on that mountain? After all who, but Moses, had really ever seen this God?"* Perhaps Moses just led them out of Egypt to make a kingdom for himself. *"And why can't God speak to all of us? There are more here than Moses who know God."*

Finally an insurrection rose up against Moses and Aaron. The man that led the insurrection was a Levitical Priest named Korah. This priest, Korah, gathered 250 renowned Princes of Israel and came to confront Moses--

As the afternoon shadows lengthened, Moses glanced at the orange streaked sky. Unconsciously, his steps picked up speed as he made his way back toward the camp. He had been in the wilderness all day fasting and seeking the face of God. His stomach rumbled at the mingled aromas of the dinner preparations. He smiled in anticipation of the dinner that he knew Zipporah was even now preparing. He was just as eager to get back to Aaron and share what words of encouragement that the Lord had spoken to him.

The men of the congregation were relaxing and the women preparing their evening meals. An old storyteller was amusing a group of spellbound children with tales of Jacob and Esau. Older children grumbled and complained about being drafted into helping the women fetch water and gather wood. The excitement that Moses felt broke forth into a radiant smile that was returned to him manifold as he hurried through the campground greeting all that he saw. As he neared the Tabernacle of Meeting Aaron came out to meet him, a look of unease creasing his brow.

"What is it?" asked Moses registering the frown on his older brother's face.

"Korah, the Levite, has requested a meeting with you."

"I've been away all day and I really must get home." Moses answered glancing in the direction of his tent where Zipporah was waiting. "I'll see him first thing in the mor--"

"He was very persistent-- said that it couldn't wait. He should be on his way to the tabernacle now." Aaron answered looking past Moses' shoulder. "That looks like him coming now...with half of Princes of Israel!"

"What?" Asked Moses turning quickly to see a crowd of men approaching with Korah at the helm. Moses smiled when he saw Korah, his friend. Korah, however, wore a frown, as did all of the men in the company. Moses and Aaron exchanged a wary glance. A knot twisted in Moses' gut. Aaron automatically moved to his brother's side. This wasn't good.

"Good afternoon Korah, friend!" Moses called out with forced cheerfulness. "What is of such great import that it brings all of you to see me after the evening sacrifice?"

"Moses...Aaron" Korah nodded still wearing a stony expression.

"Shall we go inside?" Aaron suggested. Trying to separate Korah from the company of men and win some privacy for the ensuing unpleasantness.

"Not necessary." Korah answered in clipped tones "I'll get right to the point. We all feel as though you take too much upon yourselves, seeing that the whole congregation is holy, every one of us, and the Lord is with us as well as you. Why do you set yourselves up above the congregation of the Lord?"

Moses felt as though his heart dropped to the soles of his feet. "Oh dear God, not again!" He moaned inwardly. He and Aaron both understood the view of the Lord towards rebellion. The first challenge to his authority had come from within his own household. It was an experience he would never forget. Miriam, Moses and Aaron's older sister had influenced Aaron to join with her and together they had risen up against Moses in rebellion. The Lord was so angry that He appeared in the tabernacle and Miriam was suddenly struck with leprosy. Moses pleaded with the Lord to remove the sickness from his sister. His love for her did not change even though she questioned his God-given authority. All he could think is that this was the same sister who loved him enough to weave a basket of reeds and watch over him as he sailed safely into the Pharaoh's palace where he escaped the death that many male children did not. Moses was devastated when he saw his sister's body turned white with sickness. The Lord healed her for Moses' sake. Moses' heart was grieved for his friend Korah would be judged in the same manner. God would not tolerate rebellion against his delegated authority for ultimately it was equal to rebellion against God, Himself.

"Let the Lord judge this matter. Take your censers and put fire in them. And put incense in them before the *presence of the Lord and the Lord will show who is holy. **You** take too much upon **you**, you sons of Levi. Is it a small thing to you that the Lord has called you unto Himself and has set you as stewards over his temple? He has called you near to Him to minister unto Him. This means nothing to you?" Moses answered Korah.*

"Is it a small thing that you have led us out of a land that flows with milk and honey into the wilderness to kill us? Will you also make yourself a prince over us? Does this mean nothing to you?" A voice retorted hotly.

Moses, his temper beginning to flare, spoke to the Lord saying, "Respect not their sacrifices. I have not taken one thing from them, neither have I hurt one of them!" Aaron laid a restraining hand on his brother's shoulder. There was a time when Moses' temper being provoked had led him to slay an Egyptian. These men didn't know that Moses and Aaron inwardly thanked God because his brother had learned through forty years on the backside of the mountains of Midian to follow a new leader.

Hearing the accusations being hurled against Moses and knowing the heart-rending pain that only a shepherd could know, the Lord took Moses' part. The Lord robed Himself in His glory and took the wings of the descending twilight. A blinding, ethereal light efflorescenced in the entrance of the tabernacle. The Lord was prepared to battle on the behalf of His wounded friend. The Voice that spoke was comparable to the rumble of thunder, "Separate yourselves from among this congregation, I will consume them in a moment!"

Moses' heart was torn. The Moses from forty years ago desired that these men be shown the punitive side of the God that he knew so well. How dare they question! Had not they experienced the crossing of the Red Sea? The cloud in the day and the fire in the night? What about the manna from heaven and water from the rock? What more must God do to prove that He was with them? However, at the same time there were innocent ones in the congregation. The children who were playing nearby oblivious to the deep feelings and harsh words that were being exchanged... the families who trusted Moses everyday for leadership and guidance. They would suffer for the sins of a small band of rebels. Moses fell on his face and petitioned the Lord fervently on their behalf.

"Speak to the congregation and tell them to depart from the tents of these wicked men and touch none of their belongings or you will be consumed with them." Relief washed over him like a flood as he obeyed the Lord's command.

The congregation had been slowly gathering to see what the meaning of this strange and beautiful light at the entrance of the tabernacle. Upon hearing Moses' words, they anxiously backed away from a scornful Korah and his men. As the entire congregation of Israel watched, Moses conferred with the Lord and then spoke to the congregation.

"By this you will know that the Lord has sent me to do all these works that I do, I have not done any of them of my own mind. If these men die as common men do, then the Lord has not sent me but if the ground open up and take them live into the pit then you will understand that these men have provoked the Lord."

In disbelief, the congregation began to look from one to the other trying to find confirmation that this was really happening. Was the earth really rumbling and shaking? Even as they stood trying to decide whether to flee or to stay, the ground beneath their feet began to split asunder. Suddenly Korah, his family, his tent, and all that pertained to him were swallowed up alive into the ground. Sheer panic ensued. The people began to flee fearing for their lives. Mothers snatched up children and fled. Those who could not flee, incoherently cried out to the God of Moses who stood calmly in the tabernacle entrance. The Lord had already told him what He intended. But as always Moses felt awed by the magnitude of the God that was his friend.

Although they were shaking and trembling, the priests who had stood with Korah continued to burn their incense as though their own hands were clean. They assumed that they had escaped judgment. Not until jagged shards of light tore into the now black sky and their bodies were licked with tongues of molten fire did they understand that they had wrongly assumed. Agonizing screams pierced the night as a fire from heaven consumed them.

Israel lost 250 Princes that day as once again the God of Moses had answered by fire.

Now you would think that the people would have seen that example of God's power and wrath and learned from it to honor His chosen leadership. However instead the very next day the people of God were again murmuring and complaining saying "You have killed the people of God!" Talk about missing the point! Didn't they realize that first of all Aaron and Moses couldn't have caused the ground to open up or lightening to come from the sky? The judgment that they had witnessed was God's judgment not mans. Secondly, the judgment was against rebellion, murmuring and complaining. Yet they were at this moment choosing to rebel, murmur and complain again! Again, God requested that Moses step aside while He dealt with their rebellion. Again Moses and Aaron interceded that God wouldn't kill them. God sent a plague and again a number of the children of Israel died that day for rebellion.

In His divine mercy and love, God devised a way to publicly show the rest of the Children of Israel that He had appointed their leaders. By making this point clear, God was sparing the lives of the congregation. If they listened and took heed, no further judgment would be necessary. He gave Moses these instructions: the Prince of each tribe was to inscribe his name on a rod and Moses was to place it in the Tabernacle of Meeting. The Lord instructed that Aaron's name be written upon the rod of the tribe of Levi as the Prince of the Levites. He further told Moses to leave the rods in the tabernacle overnight. In the morning, the rod of whomever He had chosen as High Priest would blossom.

It's important to realize that the rods of the princes were not newly cut branches. These rods were symbols of authority that the princes carried daily. They had been hewn from the trees long before that day. They were disconnected dead branches without the ability to in any way produce any type of foliage. The sap had long ago dried or run out of them. The only way that those dead branches could bring forth, any life would be by a supernatural act.

The next morning when Moses brought the rods out of the Tabernacle of Meeting for the entire congregation to see, Aaron's rod was the only one that budded. Not only had it budded it had actually brought forth almonds and flowers. God had reaffirmed his choice for the High Priest. All authority is ordained of God and God always supports His choice. He neither approves nor supports rebellion.

These passages also have some direct implications upon followers. God, in this situation upheld the position of his leader. Is there an instance when God upholds the position of a follower? (Not a rebel but a sincere follower) What if the leader is wrong? What does God expect of a follower?

Very simply put, the job of a follower is to learn. Everyone has the potential to lead, however, faithful service is what separates the called from the chosen. The only ones who will be exalted into a position of leadership are those who have mastered the art of following.

Dancing In The Spirit

The reward of a great follower is that he is exalted to lead. A great follower will eventually serve in the same capacity as his leader. Some good examples of this are Joseph, Joshua, Elisha, Samuel, David. Each of these men trained as servants and eventually were promoted to lead. We have seen an example of a poor follower in the preceding passage from Numbers. Now let us, again, look to David, our Old Testament Worshipper, Warrior, and King for an example.

In I Samuel, Saul is anointed King of Israel but because of grave errors during his reign, the Lord rejects Saul and anoints David to reign in his place. From the time that David was anointed King until the time that he actually reigned as King was a span of approximately fifteen years. During this time, David was a subject of Saul. He was commissioned to play for the King and he resided in Saul's palace. For slaying Goliath, David was given Michal, Saul's daughter, to wed and became the King's son-in-law and a close friend to the reigning Prince, Jonathan.

Throughout this fifteen-year time, even though David had become like a son to him, Saul grew jealous of David for many reasons. The Bible tells us that David was a good-looking young man. (I Sam 16:12) He was also very skillful in battle. Consider the fact that Goliath was challenging the entire nation of Israel, even the King himself. Rather than going out to face the giant himself, Saul offered David his amour. We can assume that David had more courage than Saul. It was noted by the women of the kingdom in their song in I Sam 18:7 extolling Saul for having killed thousands and David ten thousands. Because of his jealousy, he tried on several occasions to take David's life. The mighty King of Israel came out of his palace and pursued a youth, one of his subjects, as though he was his equal. At one point David, in anguish, cried out to Saul:

> *"After whom has the King of Israel come out? After whom doest thou pursue? After a dead dog, after a flea..."*
>
> *I Samuel 24:14*

More than once David had not just the opportunity, but also the ability to take Saul's life. All of Saul's men knew that Saul sought David's life and that he did so for no apparent reason--but Saul was king and so they followed. It was clear that David had not committed any crimes or offenses against the throne. It was clear that if he decided to stand and fight and he had slain Saul, as he would since he was the more skillful warrior, it would have been a matter of self-defense. He had just cause.

Instead, David began to live in the hills and in the caves. During this time many men who felt to be outcasts of the kingdom, joined themselves with David. He had an army of approximately 400 men who were strong and mighty in battle. Still he did not rebel. Time and time again, opportunity presented itself to be done with Saul, however, throughout the years, that Saul pursued David, David, the mighty man of war, the slayer of giants ran. David declared, "I will not put forth my hand against my lord, for he is the Lord's anointed." (I Samuel 24:10)

Even in times while our leader may not be resembling the portrait of the Good Shepherd in Psalms 23, our job is to recognize them as God's anointed. It is our job to learn. Even if the lessons are in what *not* to do.

David's example, although a hard one to follow, is our example in times of distress. And it is distress to a follower's very soul when it becomes clear that we cannot please a leader. A true follower desires to please the leader in proxy for God. We expect that our efforts will be met with at least a small appreciation. When we keep trying and meeting with opposition, it feels a little like beating your head against a brick wall.

But keep David's example before you. If you cannot please your leader make sure that you continue to please your God.

We should resolve to humble ourselves--refuse to fight back—dare not touch God's anointed, even with bitter, hasty words. (When you feel like murmuring remember Korah) Dodge spears and javelins thrown at you in the form of insults and cut-downs. Run if your life, spiritually or physically, is threatened. But until such a time, stay and learn the lesson and pass the test. Remember service, no matter the circumstances, is the training ground for leadership.

As I close this section on 'follow-ship', I would like to leave you with a snapshot of two excellent followers.

In Exodus 17:8 there is an account of how the Children of Israel lead by Joshua, made war with the Amaleks. During the battle, Moses, Hur and Aaron stood upon a hill and watched. While Moses lifted up his hands, the Children of Israel prevailed. If he dropped his hands, the Amaleks prevailed. Soon Moses became weary and he was unable to lift his arms. His followers, Aaron and Hur went and found a rock for him to sit upon. One stood on the each side and held his hands up until the going down of the sun.

Now this is a perfect picture of follow-ship. Trust and support. First, the men trusted that God was with Moses and that God had spoken to him to make war against the Amaleks. They realized that it was imperative for Moses to keep his arms up in order to complete what the Lord had given him to do. They found ways to help Moses to complete his mission.

As I studied this scripture, I realized that in order for them to help Moses to complete his mission, they had to make themselves uncomfortable. It took sacrifice. They had to find a big rock for Moses to sit upon and then move to the edge of the mountain so that he could still see the battle. Then in order to support Moses' arms they had to lift their own arms. If Moses's arms got weary, then it stands to reason that eventually theirs with the added weight of Moses' arms got heavy as well. But they persisted. The scriptures state that Moses' arms were not only lifted, but they were steady until the close of the day. These men had mastered the art of follow-ship!

Of course, today in our new covenant, God does not allow the ground to open up and swallow us, as was Korah's judgment. Christ, our High Priest, took the penalty for all of our past, present, and future errors. However, there are consequences spiritual and natural to our errors. The examples were put in scripture so that we can learn to from them. Learn to master the art of follow-ship and in due time the Lord, because he is not a respecter of peoples, will exalt you. When He does, don't forget to use your leadership role as an opportunity to give your disciples a picture of the Good Shepherd.

Lack of Leadership: The Spirit of Salome

In St. Mark 6:14-38, we are given the story of the beheading of John the Baptist. In this story, Herodias, the wife of King Herod, was incensed with John for declaring that her marriage to her husband's brother was unlawful. She asked her husband several times to have John put to death. But Herod had respect for John's ministry and refused to kill him. Herodias stood by and waited for an opportunity to fulfill her desire.

The opportunity came later when Herod commissioned, Salome, the daughter of Herodias from her first marriage, to dance for him and his guests at a birthday party. His niece's performance pleased the King so well that she was allowed to request from him anything that she wished, up to half of his kingdom. Being only a youth Salome didn't know for what to ask so she went to

Dancing In The Spirit

her mother and asked her advice. Herodias instructed her to request the head of John the Baptist on a platter. Although it grieved the king, he refused to break his promise. John was beheaded.

In this story, the girl Salome mirrors the situation of our youth today. The result of this precarious situation tends to breed problems for ministries in which they are involved. The nature of this situation has special implications for dance ministries. Let's examine Salome's situation.

1. First, she was placed in a position that she was not mature enough to handle. She was allowed to dance erotically before the King, her uncle and stepfather, and his guests.

There is another example of this in the scripture. Let's take a look. Queen Vashti, the predecessor of Queen Esther, has been depicted as a disobedient and rebellious wife because of her refusal to appear at King Ahasuerus' feast. However, in my opinion, this queen upheld the true essence of queenly grace in her refusal to obey the King's command. Some who see King Ahasuerus as a type of God would balk at this statement. However, it is difficult for me to see Ahasuerus as a type of God because although he had all authority in his realm, he was a weak King. In order to glorify himself and his riches he had a lavish party. At this party, he was drunk and commanded his beautiful queen to come and allow his drunken friends to look upon her—to further gloat in his success. Lastly, when he was disobeyed the King didn't even know what to do about it, and allowed his counselors to advise him to do something that broke his heart for he loved Vashti. God was able to use Ahasuerus's weaknesses to work His righteous plan. But I fail to see Ahasuerus as a type of God. I fail to see Vashti as rebellious and evil.

Let me explain further. How many of us as women would appear in a primarily male setting where the men had been allowed to drink until their hearts were 'merry' with wine? The way that women, especially women of great beauty, are treated at these kinds of occasions is very demeaning. It is even more unacceptable for a queen to be treated this way by her subjects and encouraged by a king who is so inebriated that he cannot demand the proper amount of respect and deference for his queen.

There is an element of 'entertainment' that is expected of women in such settings-- for instance a bachelor party. What do women usually do in these settings....dance. And in doing so they are belittled and disrespected.

Although she was not, Vashti could have been instantly beheaded for her refusal to obey Ahasuerus's command. We don't know if Salome was given the option to refuse to appear. We do know, however that quasi-incestuous act was done and sanctioned by her mother. This leads us to the second point.

2. The second problem Salome had was lack of responsible, mature leadership. Her mother had married her husband's brother. Then she allowed her daughter to perform seductively for her husband. She also selfishly used her daughter to accomplish her own demonic agenda.

Unfortunately, many ministries lack proper leadership. Either the leader is simply immature or he or is battling with their own personal issues. In the case of Salome's mother, Herodias, she was dealing with her own problems. The Spirit of Jezebel was possessing Herodias. This spirit is the mother of the Spirit of Salome.

We are first introduced to Jezebel in I Kings chapter 16 when Ahab, the son of Omri takes the throne of Israel. Instead of taking a bride of the women of Israel as the Israelites were instructed to do, Ahab marries Jezebel, a

Sidonian. According to New Unger's Bible Dictionary, the Sidonians were worshippers of Baal and Astoreth. Jezebel quickly leads Ahab and all of Israel into wickedness and idolatry. Unger's goes on to say:
> "Jezebel of infamy was daughter of Ethbaal, 'king of the Sidonians.' Her introduction of the licentious worship of Cannanite cults into Israel brought internal misery ([I Kings] 16:31-33)."

Aside from being a wicked king, Ahab is also spineless. In times of distress, he defers to his wife and abdicates his authority (I Kings 19:1, 21:1-16). Knowing her to be a worshipper of Baal and Ashtoreth, he marries her, joins her in idolatry, and leads the entire Kingdom of Israel into wickedness. As if this wasn't enough, he also allows his wife a free hand in the Kingdom to do whatever she wishes. In I Kings 18:4 we find Jezebel carrying out her satan-inspired desires by massacring the prophets of God. When the prophets of her gods are challenged and finally slaughtered by Elijah the Prophet of God, Jezebel swore by her gods to kill him. Jezebel's gods are actually demon spirits. Spirits are not limited by the concept of time and will wait eons to do their bidding.

Fourteen years after the death of her husband and after the reign of her son Jehoram, Jehu is anointed king of Israel. As Jehu rides into Jezreel to seize it, Jezebel sits in the window of her palace applying makeup. It is thought that she may have been attempting to seduce Jehu to take her as his wife after the custom of Eastern usurpers (New Unger's Bible Dictionary).

These are the fundamental characteristics of a spirit of Jezebel. She has a mission from her father Baal (satan) that gives her a driving desire to destroy Prophets of God. It is her assignment--her calling. She will use any means necessary to accomplish it. One of her favorite methods is seduction.

Jezebel was also a very controlling woman. She often took matters into her own hands when her husband vacillated. (I Kings 19:1, 21:1-16). Her desire for control also seen in her ability to direct the kingdom first through Ahab and then again during the reign of her son Jehoram.

Generations later, we are introduced to Herodias and her murderous agenda. It is ironic that the reason that she wants to kill John is because he declared her marriage unlawful. She, in the tradition of Jezebel, had seduced the new leader to take her as wife. It is even more ironic that John the Baptist is the fulfillment of the prophesy in Malachi 4:5 that Elijah would be sent back to the earth before the last days (Matt. 11:14; 17:10; Mark 9:11-13; Luke 1:17). In essence, in the spirit, Jezebel and Elijah were battling again in a different age.

Herodias however did not have the luxury of Jezebel in that she was not granted to do whatever she wished in her husband's kingdom. She wanted to control Herod however he proved to be a stronger man than Ahab, refusing to kill the Prophet of God. Moreover, her husband believed in John and respected his ministry. Being driven by demonic influences to kill John who was empowered by the spirit of Elijah, she had to resort to alternate measures.

Herodias was so driven by the Spirit of Jezebel that she took no thought for what was best even for her daughter. She was willing to allow a young, impressionable girl's innocence to be sacrificed in order to accomplish her desires. In a situation where the spirit of Jezebel could not use seduction, her favorite method, her desire to control was so all consuming that she resorted to using her own child to accomplish her purpose. The demons that possessed her cared nothing for the child only for accomplishing their purpose. Without the proper covering and protection of

Dancing In The Spirit

responsible leaders, children are vulnerable to be used as pawns. The Bible tells us that children are like arrows in the hands of a might hunter. Imagine those arrows in the wrong hands... This was Salome.

3. The girl was given a decision for which she knew she had no ability to choose wisely. In this, she deferred to her faulty leadership and was influenced to do evil.

A growing fad in child rearing today says that a child should be able to make his or her own decisions. These people are of the belief that you are to treat a child as a small adult. Children are not to be disciplined or corrected; they should just be loved and indulged. They are allowed to divorce their parents if they are not happy. Or call the Department of Children and Families if they are disciplined in a way of which they don't approve.

When I ask my nine-year-old to drive to the corner store, she'll tell me without question that she's too little to do it. On the first day of rehearsal for my very first dance ministry, I asked the young people what they wanted to do. They replied by telling me that I should tell them what to do. Their reasoning was that they had never done this before so they needed leadership. Isn't it funny that even children can tell us that they need leadership, but some psychologists still don't get it.

This is the position in which Salome found herself. Although she was given a choice, she recognized that she did not have the wisdom to make a good decision. Salome deferred to the only leadership that she had. Unfortunately it was Herodias who also had no ability to choose wisely.

I have seen youth in dance ministries given the 'right' to choose their own music, create their own choreography and design their own costumes with no supervision. This is madness! The scriptures tell us that a child left to himself will bring his mother to shame (Proverbs 29:13). Young people need supervision, direction, and boundaries. If these are not present, just like the scriptures prophesy—you will be made ashamed. Not because they will try to embarrass you, it's just that many of them are not mature enough to make the proper decisions.

We leave ourselves open to the Spirit of Salome and eventually the Spirit of Jezebel when we as leaders are weak like Ahab, or too busy with our own issues.

4. The fourth and last problem with Salome was that she was given license to display her sexuality in an unacceptable context. New Unger's Bible Dictionary tells us "the dress of the dance was planned to show the beauty of the figure to the greatest advantage." Although we know that we are not to be ashamed of our bodies, David says that we are "fearfully and wonderfully made"; we must balance this knowledge with wisdom. It is never acceptable to publicly display our sexuality. Sexuality is a good God-given privilege, but it is made for adults in marriage. There is no other proper place for sexuality.

Many teens today have leadership that is just as spiritually void in their lives. Not just in church, but especially in their homes as well. It is so critical to note that much like the situation of most young women today, Salome's father was absent. Fathers are called of God to provide a safe place for a young woman to grow naturally into her identity, even her sexual identity. It is his responsibility to provide a place where she will not be exploited or molested.

Her sexuality and its emergence is a necessary part of growing into womanhood. It is a beautiful, natural God-ordained, God-sanctioned occurrence like the blossoming of a lovely flower. In Ezekiel 16 the prophet speaks of Israel as a baby found forsaken in a field. The Lord says that he took the baby in and washed her and nurtured her. In verses 7 & 8, the text reads that her breasts developed and it became 'her time of love'. At this time, He spread His cloak over her. It is the duty of the male in authority to cover her during this most precious time of development. The Shulamite's brothers in the Song of Solomon say that their sister is a 'garden enclosed'. A woman enters the earth with a seal in her body. Only one man is permitted to break that seal in an act that occurs to seal the covenant of marriage. It is the divine responsibility of the men in a young lady's life to preserve that seal. In the absence of the father and brothers, that responsibility falls to the mother.

In the case of Salome, that God-given responsibility was forfeited and her sexuality became currency. It is painful to see that in today's society this beautiful development is still currency. Young starlets flaunt their sexuality for profit and child pornography is a million-dollar industry.

In the church, leaders who are occupied with their own problem and struggles are leading youth in many cases. As leaders, it is our responsibility to protect not only the youth but also whoever is entrusted to us from spiritual danger. Even as the Good Shepherd in Psalms 23 anointed the sheep with oil to keep bugs away. It is our responsibility to do the same for the sheep in our fold.

Young women should be allowed to grow into mature sexual beings in the time and season in which it is appropriate for them without exploitation or molestation. Of course, we all know that children are given to us to teach and train, even so in this. They should be taught that sexuality is beautiful and God-designed. It is a wonderful expression of love and covenant that has its place within the bonds of marriage. Outside of those boundaries, sensuality is not appropriate.

It is the responsibility of parents to still the voices of the media in this generation and to take their children aside and teach them the proper context of sexuality. It is the parent's responsibility to make sure that the youth is protected from being introduced to sexuality in the wrong context. There is a scripture in the Song of Solomon that says 'please do not stir or awaken my love until he pleases.' The book *Solomon on Sex* contends that this scripture alludes to the to the desire of a young person not to be sexually initiated until the proper atmosphere of marriage is created. When a child is introduced to an adult sexual situation, it is called sexual abuse.

The reason that I feel that Salome was abused in this situation is because she was not prepared to deal with the results that came of the situation. Just like the youth of today are not prepared to deal with the consequences of enticing adult men by popular suggestive dances, overly revealing clothing, or sensual attitudes being purported by their favorite celebrities. Salome had to appeal to her mother to make the ensuing decision for her. This reveals her inability to handle and make adult decisions that are a direct result of being initiated into sexual atmospheres and involvement.

When I see a young lady who is more comfortable with her sexuality than some adults, I usually associate this with a youth that has been molested or sexually abused or is presently sexually active. This is a common characteristic of youth influenced by the Spirit of Salome. Sexuality is evident in their walk, their body language, their dress, and their dance. They could be the sweetest, quietest, most amiable young people you ever want to meet however if they are emanating sexuality like a beacon, it is a red flag. They are dealing with a Spirit of Salome. They have been initiated into sexuality before they were ready and the boundaries for their sexuality have been blurred. This is not a child to be disciplined but to be taught and redirected.

Another interesting point about Salome is that she had no personal interest in having the head of John the

Dancing In The Spirit

Baptist. She had no animosity toward him. She asked for it because she was instructed to do so. Unwittingly, she allowed herself to be influenced by a spirit of seduction and then ultimately she was used by the Spirit of Jezebel to destroy a powerful Man of God. Salome had no real stake in any of it. She was simply a pawn.

I believe that this is our (dancers) position in much of this; we have no desire to destroy the character, integrity, and ministries of our brothers in Christ. We do not realize that this is what the end of our actions becomes. Not being aware doesn't cancel the consequence. The scriptures declare that we as a people are destroyed for a lack of knowledge. Just because you don't know what a gun is or the power that it has, doesn't mean that when you pull the trigger, the bullet loses it's power. Somebody is still going to get hurt.

No matter whether we want to be engaged in this spiritual battle or not, we are in it. We have to choose that either we are going to win or lose. We must choose. Not choosing is choosing.

Even if we just ignore the warnings and just conduct our dance ministry in the way that we see fit. By allowing the enemy a place no matter how small, we are leaving ourselves vulnerable to this spirit of seduction.

Identifying the Spirit of Salome:

- Do your costumes adequately cover your bodies? Are they too sheer? Are they too revealing? Are they a distraction? (i.e. breast points, panty lines, low necklines)
- Are there other serious problems evident in your dance ministry (i.e., rebellion, strife)
- Does your preparation and discussion time consist more of personal appearance (costumes, hair, jewelry) or prayer, study, & rehearsal time?

- How is your ministry received? Does it minister to the congregation? Does it lead them into worship? Does it hamper the flow of the church service?
- Does your ministry offend the mature, married women in your congregation? Is your ministry growing? Does it have a cross-section of ages and sizes and marital status?
- Is the move of the Holy Spirit evident in your ministry? How does your ministry affect the congregation? Do they seem indifferent? Do they consider dance a ministry or do they receive it as entertainment?

If you sense that something is out of order in your ministry never forget that God has given us authority over all things. All principalities, powers, and spirits are under our feet. There is nothing that the creative power in our own mouths cannot destroy using the Word of God. There are some extreme instances where it may be necessary to either scale back or completely stop the dance ministry for a season for further teaching or for fasting and prayer. If you sense that this is necessary speak with your leadership and be open to their guidance.

Some Practical Advice on Order

Dance is a very visual art. It demands attention. If you do not pay attention to it, you cannot appreciate it. However, if it is not in proper order especially in a church service, it can end up being a distraction rather than an enhancement. Therefore understanding dance's position in relation to the other parts of a church service is essential.

Unless the service itself is a dance recital, the ministry of dance is not the focal point of any service. Dance is a ministry that aids the five-fold ministry (see Ephesians 4:12) to accomplish its purpose which is to perfect the saints for the working of the ministry.

The first purpose of the dance ministry is to provide another medium by which the Body receives from the heart of God. Dance and any other art form can also be used to reinforce the message from the pulpit. It also adds the dimension of visual learning of the scriptures by providing not only hearing but visual demonstrations.

Additionally, the dance ministry helps to promote member-to-member relationships in the local body by requiring members to work together in close proximity to produce effective ministry productions. Many areas of necessary growth are not realized until working relationships are formed. When members work together, spiritual maturity is the outcome. Proverbs 27:17 tells us that as iron sharpens iron and friends sharpen friends. By rubbing iron against iron, sharpening occurs thus by working and or fellowshipping together sharpening of men occurs.

In addition, as relationships are formed it is less likely that members will fall through the cracks. When members have friends in the church and are doing something that they feel is productive they are more likely to be loyal and committed to their ministries and less likely to get lost in the crowd or feel disconnected.

Finally, the dance ministry will help to mature and develop the gifts of talented members by providing 'on the job' training and experience. The arts are an extremely effective evangelism tool especially to youth. The dance ministry will train lay people to be ministers that flow in God's anointing and communicate the heart of God to the body of Christ as a whole as well as to a lost world. Some of the specific purposes of the dance ministry are to:

- Expand upon the truths of the Bible that comes across the pulpit by presenting it in a fresh new form

- Introduce and teach the new believer the progression of Praise to Worship for use in his personal life

- Create an atmosphere of liberty, freedom and joy that encourages the believer to lay aside their cares and enter into the presence of the Lord

- Provide an arena where Christians can use their gift of dance in the Lord's house and not feel that there is no outlet for Christian performers

- Use the gifts and talents outside the walls of the church to reach out to those who have yet to come into a relationship with Christ

- To assist in creating an atmosphere of praise and worship that will whet the congregations appetite for God and cause rivers of living water to flow

There are a few tips that I would like to submit to you with respect to dance in its proper order in the church. There are many guidelines where it comes to dance, some are my personal preferences, and some are general church etiquette.

- It is always good in any ministry to have a *designated* leader. Having a specified leader eliminates much confusion and strife from the onset. The leader must be someone who is mature, trustworthy, and skilled.
- If you are the leader for your church's dance ministry before you begin, it is a good idea to sit down and prayerfully write out your expectations for the members. Is it okay to miss rehearsals without calling? Is there a training period during which a new dancer will sit and observe? What are

Dancing In The Spirit

the reasons that someone might be released from the dance ministry?

- Dancers must be trained on the times to move and to be still. There should be no movement during prayers, altar calls, and sermons unless the Pastor has granted prior approval.

It is best not to give new or young dancers the liberty to judge these times. To do this is to trust that everyone in the dance ministry is mature enough to decide when to dance and when not to. Although this is what we are striving for, it is not always so. It should be at the discretion of the Dance Leader, submitted to Pastoral authority that the dancers are taught the appropriate times to dance or to be still for that local body. As the dancers grow and learn to flow in the Spirit, they too will be able to sense when it is okay to move.

- Costumes for a dance ministry must be chosen very carefully. In order for costumes to be decent and in order, they must be modest. Modest in this sense does not necessarily mean understated. Sequins, lame, tassels, and other fancy notions are fine for a dance ministry. By modest I more refer to the cut, weight, and function of the cloth.

This is a very tough subject because there are many Christian dancers that don't agree that there should be marked difference between dance attire Christian dancers and for secular dancers. As we discussed in earlier chapters, the ministry of dance is very vulnerable to being presented in error and therefore becomes very vulnerable to being dismissed as something that is not for the church. We as ministers using dance must remember that our first and foremost concern is to minister life and convey the heart of God. If the costume in any way distracts from that purpose, it is counter-productive.

Karen M. Curry

Leotards are usually tight, clingy and sometimes see through. Although they are accepted secular dance attire, special precautions must be made in conforming them to church use. Most dance ministries like to use white because it is such an appropriate color to symbolize purity, holiness, and cleanliness. In leotards, however, white can be very sheer. It is never appropriate for bras to show through leotard fabric or for breasts to point through. I have found that an easy solution to both problems is to incorporate a light vest to your dance costume. They look very nice especially in lame or other festive fabrics and they are very easy to sew.

It is equally distracting for white panties or bikini panty lines to show through light colored dance skirts. A solution for this is to incorporate a dance slip to your wardrobe. A good idea for a dance slip is to use a pair of very wide culottes so that even if the skirt ends up around your waist you are still covered underneath.

Jewelry or long, brightly painted nails can be another distraction. If you happen to dance with ladies who wear a lot of chains, rings, earrings and bracelets, or long, painted nails it sometimes tends to distract from the Object of our worship. It is a good idea to have the dancers remove excessive jewelry and or revert to clear or understated nail colors before dancing in order to keep the focus where it should be.

If we agree on our purpose, which is to bring glory and honor to God, these would be small steps to take in order to assure that this is done.

VIII. The Priestly Office

In the scriptures the singers, dancers, musicians, ushers, and even the people who cleaned the temple bathrooms were all a part of a special family who was set apart by God to conduct the temple business. (Numbers 1:50 & 51) This family was the comprised of the descendants of Levi, who was the third son of Jacob and Leah. If you read the story of Leah, you will find that she was unloved by her husband. For the blessing of giving him a third son she hoped to be joined to him thus she named the child Levi which means 'joined to'.

She waited and hoped for that joining but her desire for Jacob's heart went unrequited. Her fourth and last child she named Judah meaning 'praise'. Instead of becoming bitter in her disappointment, Leah set her heart to praise and worship God instead. Being the all-knowing all-seeing God that He is, God found pleasure in her ability to satisfy herself in Him. Although she was never joined to Jacob, God Himself joined Himself to her offspring forever in a most intimate fashion. Not only were the Levites a divine order of priests separated and holy unto God, but also Jesus Christ God's own son was a descendant of Leah's as the "Lion of the Tribe of Judah".

The Levites were chosen by God to be His separate possession, and they served as a tithe or first fruits of the people who were called out of Egypt.

> And I, behold, I have taken the **Levites** from among the children of Israel instead of all the firstborn that openeth the matrix among the children of Israel: therefore the **Levites** shall be mine;
>
> Num 3:12

Much like the children of Israel were chosen from among all of the people of the world--so it is with all of us. Even more so like us, the Levites had no input or choice in their calling. The decision was God's divine sovereignty. In His omniscience, He decided that the Levites were the people that would minister in the temple. Thus, they were given to Aaron as a gift to assist in the duties of the priesthood. (Numbers 3:9, 8:19).

A Levite began his service in the temple at the age of 25 and was retired at the age of 50. (Num 8:24 & 25) They had no income or inheritance so the Children of Israel were commanded to bring a tithe (or tenth) of their income to the temple to support the Priests and Levites. (Num 18:23 & 24) Several times in scripture, Moses received offerings of the congregation and gave them to the Levites. (Num 7:6, 31:47) Although they received no inheritance, of land, they were given suburbs. (Num 35:6, Josh 21:8, 21:27, I Chron 6:64)

The specific jobs of the Levitical Priesthood were many. Some included assisting with the sacrifices and offerings (II Chron 29:24), keeping the temple treasure (I Chron 9:26), maintaining incense on the altar, baking and refreshing the showbread (II Chron 13:10), instructing in and delivering the law (II Chron 35:3), guarding the temple (II Chron 23:4) and serving as scribes (II Chron 34:13).

As we follow the Levites history in scripture, it seems as though although they were first given to Aaron and his sons as servants, they later became sect of priests in their own right. Starting in around II Chronicles the phrase, "the priests and the Levites" became quite common. It seems that their identity became almost fused with the priests and that their duties became more elevated. Under the reign of King David, the Levites were also given a rest and were no longer required to carry the Ark of the Covenant. (I Chron 23:25 & 26) In addition, during David's reign the Levites were appointed servants to assist them in the temple duties called the Nethinims. (Ezra 2:70)

The Levites, whom I also call the *'Priests of Praise'*, were also best known noted for their skill with music and song. The first call for musicians to minister before the Ark of God came in II Chronicles 15 when David appoints the Levites to cleanse themselves and prepare to carry the Ark of the Covenant correctly. He instructs them to appoint singers and musicians from among themselves to serve for this historical event.

When asked by the Levites to provide a minister of music, Asaph was one of the select few. (I Chron 15:17) Asaph, a Chief Levite, to whom is accredited many of the Psalms, along with his brothers provided the music and singing on that celebrated day. (It would seem that musical families were evident long before the Winans and the Clark Sisters!) They were later appointed by David to minister around the clock before the Ark of the Covenant. (I Chron 16:37)

The descendants of Asaph are also noted for their musical skill. Later in scripture rather than Asaph and his brothers, the phraseology became Asaph and his sons. Later Levites and music ministers were labeled as sons of Asaph. (I Chron 26:1, II Chron 20:14, Ezra 2:41, Ezra 3:10, Neh 7:44, Neh. 11:22). And although Asaph is first mentioned as 'Asaph the recorder' merely writing the events as he was instructed to do, he is later dubbed 'Asaph the seer' who was a prophet seeing and speaking heavenly things himself. Asaph embodied the example of a true worshipper by duplicating his spirit in his disciples.

Aaron the High Priest and his sons comprised another order of priests called the Aaronic Priesthood. This priesthood represents today's five fold ministry or church leadership: Apostles, Prophets, Evangelists, Pastors and Teachers - Ephesians 4:11. Ephesians 4:12 tells us that the mission of the five-fold ministry is to equip the saints to do the work of the ministry.

It is the job of the Levitical Priesthood to uphold and under-gird the mission of the Aaronic Priesthood. This is our God-given priestly duty. Apart from the five-fold ministry, our message is incomplete. If we break up the fallow ground in their hearts, and prepare them to receive the message from God, who then will stand up and deliver it? We can dance until the Spirit of God falls but who then would teach the people how to respond to this atmosphere? Who would declare to them what the Lord is saying in the atmosphere that we have created? Once the anointing that is created through our praise breaks the yokes and fetters off of their lives, who would walk with them day by day until they learn break the chains by themselves? This is the function Aaronic Priesthood--to equip and mature the saints of God to do the work of the ministry.

One plows, one waters, and God gives the increase.

Shall we defer to the Ox-Cart?

As Levitical Priests, it is an honor and a privilege to carry the anointing of God upon our shoulders. Just like the priests of old, we true worshippers are a called out group. We are God's special possessions. We are not content to visit the temple on Sundays. We instead pitch our tents close because we desire to always be close to His Presence. We are the ones who keep the incense burning on the altar of God even through the midnight hours. We take comfort in the shadow of the wings of the cherubim. The Mercy Seat is our refuge. We see it as a sublime joy. Our calling; our life.

There is another point that is made by the illustration of the transport of the Ark of the Covenant in I Kings. Remember the ill-fated move that caused a breach upon the Children of Israel? (I Chron 13:11, 15:13) We know that Uzzah died for touching the Ark. But have you ever stopped to wonder why the Ark was on the ox-cart in the first place? The Levites are trained from their youth to know and understand their duties in the temple of God. Even if King David, who was not a Levite, did not understand the law, why would they allow such an error to occur? They were the teachers, scribes, and keepers of the law. They knew better!

Well let us think about it.... Have you ever considered how heavy that Ark must have been? Gold is one of the heaviest materials on earth. The acacia wood of which the Ark was constructed was gold plated inside and out. There were solid gold cherubim of beaten gold atop the lid, which was also gold. Even the staves, which were inserted into the golden rings, were gold-covered acacia wood. It had to be heavy! Maybe the priests thought of David "If he doesn't know any better, we won't tell him!" Perhaps they were happy to put what belonged on their shoulders—which speaks of responsibility—upon an ox-cart. Maybe what should have been a privilege and a joy had become a burden.

If we are not careful, the Presence of God even in our lives today can be seen as a weight and a burden rather than a joy. The fact that God placed it upon the shoulders of the priests reveals that it was to be seen as a responsibility. However, through the eyes of a worshipper this responsibility is a precious one much like the weight of an unborn child in the womb of its mother--or the responsibility of a husband to care for his wife and children. Some responsibilities are so sweet that they can hardly be compared to burdens. So it is with the responsibility of carrying God's anointing to the true worshipper.

However, our flesh loves to be comfortable and resists exertion of any kind. So in order to accommodate our flesh we resist carrying the Ark. Instead of embracing the holiness that is necessary in order to carry the full manifestation of the power and presence of God, we choose a halfhearted, quazi-holiness that denies the power of God in its fullness. In order for us to fully accept our priesthood, we force God to take us through a process that causes our Uzzah (flesh or human strength) to die.

King David once made the statement "I would not offer my God something that costs me nothing." (I Chr 21:24) The priesthood will cost you. There is time that will be invested whether it is pouring into others or developing your skill. There is sometimes sleep that will be lost as you keep the midnight incense burning in the temple. Sometimes you will sacrifice your comfort lying prostrate or kneeling. Even money will be sacrificed to develop and cultivate your skill or to support the ministry in which you are involved. Beloved, trust me as you get hungrier—more desperate, the sacrifices will be multiplied. There will come a day when He will ask you for what is dearest to your heart. Just ask Abraham.

So, just between you and me--what keeps you from fully embracing your calling? Shall we eliminate the obstacles or shall we bring out the ox-cart? How much are you willing to let go of? How much more of Him do you desire? What are you willing to do to be closer to Him?

In the book of Exodus the Children of Israel grew weary of waiting for Moses to return from Mt. Sinai where he was getting instruction from God. Lead by Aaron they fashioned a golden calf to worship. When Moses returned and found them in the reveling, wild act of idolatry his response is "Who is on the Lord's side come to me."

Dancing In The Spirit

The Sons of Levi respond by gathering to Moses. Moses then instructs the Sons of Levi to go forth and execute those who were participating in the idolatry. These were kinsmen, dear to their hearts, people that they had grown up with, played with, and worshipped with. Yet, in order to preserve their union with God a critical choice had to be made. The question is what are you willing to kill? Habits and thought systems that you've been nurturing and maintaining from childhood? Friendships and relationships that are dear to your heart? How badly do you want Him? Can you bear the weight of pure gold on your shoulders or do I hear the rattle of wagon wheels….perhaps an ox-cart?

Within the Levitical Priesthood, there was a smaller sect, a chosen few called the Kohathites, who were given the actual duty of carrying the Ark. Even today within the worshippers, a smaller set actually gets the honor of getting closer than anyone else. No, this is not favoritism on God's part. He is no respecter of persons however He did predestine each of us to our expected end. God who knows the intents and purposes of the heart also knows the end from the beginning. He knows within whose heart resides the desire, the passion and the perseverance to press their way into the Holy of Holies. Is it you? Are you determined…. or shall we prepare the ox-cart?

Oxen are known as 'beasts of burden'. It is their job to push pull or carry, anything that is too heavy for us or perhaps not too heavy but too much bother—not worthy of our exertion or our sweat. God is extending to His special possessions, you and I, an opportunity to be close to His manifest presence to bear it about upon our bodies. In scripture, the ones closest to Him chose instead to put His manifest presence upon an ox-cart. Yes, the responsibility is heavy. Yes, the sacrifices are many—even above that which is necessary to salvation. The invitation has gone out—the very God of the Universe, the Creator of all Life has issued an invitation sealed in blood to come closer, will you accept the call or shall we defer to the oxen?

VI. The Progression

It is God's desire that we worship Him. Not only does He dwell in our praise but in our worship we are changed into His image. However, because He knows that we are not able to reach Him, He has prescribed a pattern for us to be able to come near to Him. The pattern is the tabernacle for which God gave Moses the blueprint on Mt. Sinai. This pattern is essential if we want to understand the progression of praise into worship. And it is only in worship that we can get as close to God as our burning hearts desire. Each phase of praise and worship is birthed out of the previous one. As the worshipper grows spiritually and as his/her relationship with the Lord deepens they understand and begin to move from one phase and into the next.

Below is the terminology that I use so in order to be on the same page going forward I'll define them for you. Although the first two terms are quite self-explanatory, the second two may be new terms for some:

- *group* - more than one dancer
- *solo* - one dancer
- *choreographed* - the dance was created and rehearsed in advance
of the presentation
- *spontaneous* - the dance is being created as it is presented; unrehearsed

Referring to the diagram on in The Appendix, please note that there are three sections of the Tabernacle of Moses: the outer court, the inner court and the Holy of Holies. This three-part or triune structure is patterned after man, who is composed of body, soul and spirit. Man is made is the image of God who is also a triune being consisting of the Father, Son and Holy Ghost.

Karen M. Curry

The Outer Court - Praise Dance

At the beginning of our journey into the Lord's presence, we enter the outer court. In the diagram of the Tabernacle of Moses, the outer court is the largest of the three-part structure. There were two articles in the outer court: the brazen altar and the bronze laver. Sacrifices were made upon the brazen altar and the laver was used as a washing place for the priests after the sacrifices were made. (Exodus 30:28, 39:39, Malachi 1:7, 12)

The 100th Psalm tells us that we must enter into His courts with praise. Rather than bulls or goats, praise is the sacrifice that we offer God today. It requires putting aside of all of our disappointments, all of our hurts, and every weight that might keep us from approaching Him. It requires pressing into the frame of mind that chooses to go beyond what we feel and giving thanks to God even when we would rather not. Remember David saying, "Bless the Lord, O my soul" (Psalms 103:1)? The soul is the area of man that houses his feelings, his mind, and his emotions. Perhaps that day David's feelings and emotions were in tune with his spirit's desire to honor God. He offered a sacrifice of praise and commanded his soul to come into agreement with him.

As we enter into the outer court, we find the atmosphere of celebration. There are many people, all singing and dancing. We find the saved and the unsaved, the bound and the free; we find demon and angelic spirits. Everyone can enter here. No one is alienated. The Lord has ordained praise even out of the mouths of babes and sucklings. (Psalms 8:2) Anyone can do it.

The most elementary type of liturgical dance is praise dance. It is usually choreographed, group dance. However, as in most cases an element of freedom can be added by letting go of the choreography. In most cases (but not always) praise music is happy, bouncy music that thanks God for what He has done or for what we believe He will do. Therefore, the corresponding dances are happy, bouncy dances that are constantly moving and encouraging the congregation to lay down their cares and enter into the Lord's court.

In this instance, a praise dancer is much like a cheerleader. Miriam exemplifies this type of dance at the crossing of the Red Sea in Exodus 15. Again, Miriam is not satisfied with praising the Lord alone. She encourages the spectators to become participators in extolling God for his miraculous deliverance.

The prophet Isaiah declares that God has given us the garment of praise for the spirit of heaviness. The praise dance is the medicine that lifts a spirit of gloom off of a congregation that is too heavy to enter into praise. The praise dance is also effective in your prayer closet to dispel a spirit of gloom from your own life. In fact, it is a good idea to master it in your prayer closet first. Learn to use your slingshot in the wilderness before you face Goliath!

The Inner Court (The Holy Place) - Worship Dance

As we make our way into the inner court, the atmosphere changes ...and the crowds dwindle. There is an atmosphere of quiet reverence. Before we can enter into the Holy Place, we are required to stop by the bronze laver. Here, because the laver was constructed of mirrors, we were required to see ourselves, recognize any dirt and filth, and wash before entering the presence of the King. Those who choose not to wash in the laver will remain in the outer court. No matter how many CDs or DVDs or books or concert tickets they sell, they will only know the God of the outer court. Don't get me wrong there is a need for priests to stand in the outer court to help usher new believers in, but even those priests, if they are true worshippers will have a desire to see what lies ahead—to get a little closer to that divine, heavenly light that rests between the cherubim. A true worshipper would never be satisfied until he got closer.

Some saints have learned to mask their pain under the cover of the loud music. They have learned to hide the tears in the fast paced atmosphere of praise. These things: the masks and the noise are left outside in the outer court, washed away by the cleansing of the bronze laver. The ones who are not yet ready to stand uncovered with the Almighty are absent in worship because in worship all is uncovered. There is no hiding place. Worship is standing naked before God and allowing not only Him but also sometimes all present to see your most tender places. There is no pain in the heart that is left unexplored; the skeletons in the closet are on display. This is why the best worship experiences are had in private prayer closets. Don't cheat yourself out of that experience with God. You never really know Someone until you've pulled away from the crowd and spent time alone with them. That is when communion is heart to heart and face-to-face.

In worship, you alone stand before God sometimes with tears running down your face as you whisper to Him the secrets of your heart in a rush of incomprehensible syllables of some heavenly language. You feel exposed, you feel vulnerable. All of your emotions and feelings and hurts and wounds are laid open for inspection. But as you learn to worship you become oblivious to the fact that anyone else can see your heart. You realize only that you are communing with God; your soul is speaking directly to Him. You are expressing your love to Him and your soul feels as if it would faint with the joy of it. Beloved, this is what we live for!

The furnishings of the Holy Place are the golden candlestick, the table of shewbread, and the altar of incense.

(Exodus 40:22, I Chronicles 9:22, Exodus 40:24, Exodus 37:25-28, 40:5) All of these things speak of relationship. The candlestick was representative of seven New Testament churches, the Bride of Christ. The shewbread was only to be partaken of by those who had relationship with God-- the priests who were His special possession. The altar of incense was representative of the prayers of the saints rising before the throne of God as a sweet smelling savor. Again, this speaks of those who have personal relationship with Him. The ones that enter into the Holy Place are true seeker of His heart—the ones who have persevered, the ones who were desperate.

This is not a place for everyone. Not everyone would do what it takes to make it in. Not everyone is willing to be exposed and vulnerable. No one is willing to stop by that laver and not only see their faults and flaws but choose to confess them and wash them away. By seeing your filth and recognizing your inability to remove it, humility, dependence and brokenness is birthed in earnest in the heart. True gratefulness and earnest worship causes elders and bishops, kings and princes to cast down their golden crowns at His feet.

Worship dances are also either solo or group, choreographed or spontaneous dances depending upon whether the dance is a special full-length presentation or a part of a Sunday praise & worship service. If the dance is a full-length special group presentation, it should be choreographed and rehearsed. As it is choreographed, it should be true to the message of the song. This makes the selection of a song vital. The dance should convey the desire for God, the hunger, the passion the persistence, the pursuit.

If it is a part of a praise and worship service, it is preferable to allow the worship time for individual dancers to express themselves in worship. It is a good idea to encourage them to be free enough to try spontaneous dance. Worship dancing is an ideal way to learn spontaneous dance because the essence of worship is expression of the heart. Thus, a new dancer can feel confident knowing that she is only being asked to express her heart, not to remember choreography, execute technique, or impress anyone. It is personal; no one is judging.

Holy of Holies - Prophetic Dances

As we enter into the Holy of Holies, we find a dimly lit chamber. Before the sacrifice of Jesus, a thick veil separated this part of the tabernacle. No one was allowed to enter. Even the high priests, who came in once a year to make the atonement for the nation, would drop dead in the presence of God if there was any sin in their life. When they entered behind the veil, they were outfitted with little bells attached to their clothing and a rope around their waist. If the bells stopped ringing the people knew that they would have to use the rope that had been tied around the priest's waist to pull him out from behind the veil.

The only furnishing is the Ark of the Covenant. (Numbers 10:33, Exodus 25:22). Atop the Ark was the Mercy seat. This is the place where God promised Moses that He would meet with him.

> And there I will meet with thee, and I will commune with thee from above the mercy seat, from between the two cherubims which [are] upon the ark of the testimony, of all [things] which I will give thee in commandment unto the children of Israel.
>
> Exd 25:22

He promised that He would commune with Moses and give him commandments for Israel. The same holds true for us.

In the Holy of Holies, you have finished expressing. You are quiet; you are still. There is nothing more to say. He talks and we quietly listen. He reveals to you the secrets of His Kingdom. He shares wisdom with you that brings wealth and health to your life. This is the place where we get our instructions for our flock or our disciples or our employees or our businesses or our ministries. The ideas that spark multi-million dollar companies are here. Whispered words of comfort to soothe broken hearts are here. This is the most abundant place in existence because He speaks here. But we have to know the pattern in order to get here!

Its funny that at the end (or at least the highest place I know) of this progression, we're still. We don't dance in this place. We don't preach or sing in this place. That's why this pursuit cannot be a pursuit to become a better dancer or singer or musician or preacher. It has to be a pursuit for Him. It has to be desperately striving for Him. Once we've gotten to this place, we listen and what we hear we take back outside. Sometimes it goes to the outer court much more often it goes even further outside of the temple walls and into the world.

When we take words, songs, or images of life and comfort and peace from the Mercy Seat and broadcast them to the church and to the world beyond our doors, this is prophetic ministry. Don't be confused by the term 'prophetic' or 'prophesy'. Prophecy does not always mean telling the future. Sometimes it does. However, a more accurate definition of prophetic would be speaking the heart or mind of God right now. What is God saying or feeling or thinking right now?

I don't want to injure some people's theology but do you realize that God didn't suddenly become mute when John the Revelator died? God continues to speak to His people even today, even right now! The Bible is and will always be the infallible revelation of God and by it we will always prove and measure what we hear today but God is still speaking. We are to live by every word that proceeds out of the mouth of God. His word is still proceeding! Do you know what God is saying today? Do you know what He said yesterday? Only by communing with Him will we ever know.

As dancers, after we have heard His heart and His mind when we go out of our prayer closets we create and present dances—visual, fluid, poetic pictures that give snapshots into the mind of God today—right now. We show people through visual artistic expressions what God is saying about them, about their lives, about their troubles, about their futures. This is prophetic dance. In this, we have become an avenue for God to speak His heart today—in real time.

Not every one presses their way into the Holy of Holies. Not all dancers will concern themselves with conveying God's heart. Some dancers will dance for years in the outer court and be content there. Some will dance there forever and never learn that there is more. I am aware that there are things that I have not learned yet concerning this progression. But I have learned this—every time I feel like I've gotten closer to Him, He lets me know that I'm so much further than I thought I was. In his book, "The God Catchers" Tommy Tenney calls this game 'hidey face'. God hides Himself, careful to leave a breadcrumb trail—just so that we will search for Him. Every now and then, we find Him and have an experience like no other in His presence. Then He'll move and the desperate pursuit begins all over again.

When I first started searching for Him, I didn't understand why He was hiding from me. I would explode into heart-wrenching tears thinking that I was doing something wrong—that I was so sinful and so inadequate and that He would not come and commune with me. That is a lie, don't believe it—press your way into the inner court and further into the Holy of Holies. It took me years to understand that He's going to show up. He's always going to come—always. If you seek you will find. If you knock it will be opened to you.

It's His pleasure to show up. He loves to commune with us. Remember in order for living waters to flow in the streets of your community and beyond they've got to start in your belly! He's going to come we don't know when He'll show up. It may be the first time you pray it may be the 100th but He's coming! When He comes it is to the persistent, to the hungry, to the desperate. Don't be content with the outer court; don't get stuck in the holy place. There's more—there's so much more!

We must continue to seek His face until living water runs through the streets of our neighborhoods, cities and nations.

Appendix

The Tabernacle of Moses

THE HOLY OF HOLIES

THE LAVER

THE HOLY PLACE

THE BRONZE ALTAR

Bibliography

Law, Terry. The Power of Praise and Worship. Victory House Publishers, 1985

Nance, Terry. God's Armorbearer. Harrison House

Cornwall, Judson. Worship As David Lived It. Revival Press, 1990

Landsman, Dr. Michael. Supportive Ministries. 1979

Laird, Charlton. Webster's New World Dictionary. Wiley, John & Sons, Incorporated, 1995

Unger, Harrison, Vos, Barber. Unger's Bible Dictionary. Moody Press, 1988

Sproul, R.C.. The Holiness of God. Tyndale Publishers, 1985

Tenney, Tommy. God's Favorite House. Destiny Image Publishers, 2000

Tenney, Tommy. The God Catchers. Destiny Image Publishers, 2000

Dillow, Joseph E. Solomon on Sex. Thomas Nelson 1982

About the Author:

Karen M. Curry graduated in 1993 from Florida A&M University with a major in Economics and a minor in Theatre. During her stay in Tallahassee, Ms. Curry served as a dancer with Wings of a Dove Dance Ministry of Metropolitan Cathedral of Truth from 1988 to 1991. After leaving Tallahassee in 1993, she had the privilege of planting dance ministries for several Central Florida area churches starting with Victorious Living Fellowship in 1993. During this time, she also worked with at-risk, inner city youth first as a Dance Instructor and later as Director of Dance and Theatre for the Frontline Outreach ministry.

After working in the career college industry for 5 years, in January 2004 Ms Curry resigned her position as Vice-President of a local university. Having founded The 911 Project, a Christ-centered worship arts organization that uses the performing arts to mentor at-risk youth, Ms. Curry is serving in full-time ministry. www.911-Project.org. A native of Mims, Florida, Ms. Curry currently resides in Bradenton, Florida with her two children Loren and Simone Curry where she is a member of Abundant Life Christian Center.

Printed in the United States
49231LVS00001B/20